Illustrated by Merrily Harpur, and introduced by Jill Tweedie (who also writes regularly for the *Guardian*), the *Letters from a Fainthearted Feminist* offer the uncomprehending an insight into those issues which trouble so many women – and the Sisterhood the reminder that, for many, the spirit may be willing but the flesh is weak.

Letters From a Fainthearted Feminist

Introduced by Jill Tweedie

Illustrated by Merrily Harpur

published by Pan Books

Grateful thanks to the *Guardian*,
where these letters first appeared.

First published 1982 by Robson Books Ltd
This Picador edition published 1983 by Pan Books Ltd,
Cavaye Place, London SW10 9PG
© Jill Tweedie 1982
ISBN 0 330 26908 9
Printed and bound in Great Britain by
Collins, Glasgow.

Introduction

Martha and Mary have been soul mates of mine for more years than I can count. Well, I can count them actually – I'm not daft you know – but I do not choose to at this moment in time. All three of us are deeply committed to the principles of the Women's Movement. That is to say, Martha's committed, Mary's committed and I'm committed, though none of us is entirely convinced of the ideological correctness of the others' commitment. Not that we make a thing about it, obviously, being Sisters. We just talk occasionally among ourselves. For instance, Martha might say to me that it's all very admirable, she's sure, Mary carrying on like she's Boadicea, but she (Martha) cannot help noticing that she (Mary) keeps a very low profile when it comes to the question of men, children and families generally, which is a bit odd since that's where feminism's front line is, if you come right down to it, right?

Whereas Mary might point out to me that if Martha really rejected housework and the patriarchal society as completely as she (Mary) has, she (Martha) would have downed brooms and booted out a certain patriarch who shall be nameless long ago, not to mention the fact that it's no good calling yourself a feminist without having a political dimension. Also, I happen to know that both of them get together behind my back now and then and point out to each other that me being a wage slave and a paid-up wife and houseperson means I've capitulated to the Superwoman put-down, which is hardly the royal road to women's liberation, is it?

Mary once mentioned that the seminal influence on her feminism was Valerie Solanas, the woman who shot Andy Warhol in the sixties, wrote the S.C.U.M. Manifesto (Society for Cutting Up Men) and advocated women's total separatism. And Martha once told me that her seminal influence was Betty Freidan, author of *The Feminine Mystique*, who is rather keen on women in the family, all things being equal. Personally, I think that says something about the level of both their consciousnesses – how can two feminists talk about seminal influences when the word is clearly 'ovarian'? My own ovarian influences are Valerie Solanas and Betty Freidan, which is why I am forced to retire, once or twice a year, to quiet cottage hospitals in country surroundings.

I first came across Martha's letters when I was staying for a few days with Mary at Sebastopol Terrace. They were being used to prop up Mary's kitchen table at the time because it only had three and a half legs. I unwedged and read them in between meals, which gave me plenty of time to absorb them because Mary doesn't go in a whole lot for what are generally called meals. And I thought, when I'd finished them, that other women in Martha's situation might like to read them too, if only to check out their feelings *vis-à-vis* hers. So, with Martha's permission, I suggested their publication and this is them. These are they. Mary's letters to Martha, in case you were wondering, ended up in Martha's cat's litter tray.

Before I close, I should like to make my own position clear. I have often been irritated by Martha's fainthearted approach to feminism (I am not at all like that, myself) and I must say I often deplore Mary's blinkered fundamentalism (I am not at all like that, myself). I'm sure that sensible readers will agree with me that the way ahead for women is an amalgam of the two. A faintheartedness tempered with fundamentalism. Or is it a fundamental faintheartedness? You pays your money and you takes your choice. Women's liberation is, after all, about choice.

1982   Jill Tweedie

Dear Mary

Sorry I haven't written for a while, but back here in Persil Country the festive season lasts from November 1 (make plum pudding) to January 31 (lose hope and write husband's thank-you letters). I got some lovely presents. A useful Spare Rib Diary. A book called The Implications of Urban Women's Image in Early American Literature. A Marks and Sparks rape alarm. A canvas Backa-Pak so that the baby can come with me wherever I go – a sort of DIY rape alarm. And, of course, your bracing notelets, which will be boomeranging back to you for the rest of the year. Things I did not get for Christmas: a Janet Reger nightie, a feather boa, a pair of glittery tights.

Looking back, what with God Rest Ye Merry Gentlemen, Good King Wenceslas, Unto Us a Son is Born, We Three Kings, Father Christmas ho-hoing all over the place and the house full of tired and emotional males, I feel like I'm just tidying up after a marathon stag party. Our Lady popped up now and again but who remembers the words to her songs once they've left school? We learnt them but, then, ours was an all-girl school, in the business of turning out Virgin Mother replicas. If I ever get to heaven, I'll be stuck making manna in the Holy Kitchens and putti-sitting fat feathered babies quicker than I can say Saint Peter. Josh, on the other hand, will get a celestial club chair and a stiff drink. If God is a woman, why is She so short of thunderbolts?

I went to a fair number of parties dressed up as Wife of Josh but, to tell you the shameful truth, it was my Women's Collective beanfeast that finally broke my nerve. One wouldn't think one could work up a cold sweat about going as oneself to an all-woman party, would one? One can. I had six acute panic attacks about what to wear, for a start. Half my clothes are sackcloth, due to what Josh still calls my menopausal baby (come to me, my menopausal baby) and the other half are ashes, cold embers of the woman I once was. Fashion may well be a tool of women's oppression but having to guess is worse. In the end I went makeup-less in old flared jeans and saw, too late, that Liberation equals Calvin Klein and Lip Gloss or Swanky Modes and Toyah hair but not, repeat not, Conservative Association jumble. Misery brought on tunnel vision, I swooned like a Victorian lady and had to be woman-handled into a taxi home. Quelle fiasco.

That same evening, the blood back in my cheeks, I complained to Josh that I was cooking the three hundred and sixtieth meal of 1980 and he said move aside, I'll take over. Coming to, I found myself, family and carry-cot in a taxi driving to a posh restaurant. Very nice, too, but Josh was so smug afterwards that I felt it incumbent upon me, in the name of Wages for Housework, to point out that his solution to the domestic chore-sharing problem had just cost us fifty quid, and if he intended to keep that up, he'd have to apply for funding to the IMF. Bickered for the rest of the evening, Josh wittily intoning his Battle of Britain speech – you can please some of the women all of the time and all of the women . . . but you know the rest, ha ha.

I had hardly recovered from these two blows to the system when Mother arrived to administer her weekly dose of alarm and despondency. How can I *think*, she said 18 times, of letting my Daughter drive van, alone, to Spain? Do I *want* her to be raped, mutilated and left for dead in foreign parts? It is my duty to insist that a *man* goes with her. I point out that Jane is a large, tough, 20-year-old rather more competent than me, Mother and Mother's Husband put together and Mother leaves room in huff. I then had a panic attack about Jane being raped, mutilated and left for dead in foreign parts and insisted she took a man with her. Like the Yorkshire Ripper, you mean, shouted Jane and left room in huff.

Myself, I blame British Rail. Does Sir Peter Parker realize the mayhem caused to family units all over Britain by pound-a-trip Grans intent on injecting overdue guilt into long-unvisited daughters? Josh's Ma trained over, too, apparently to make sure I wouldn't grass on Josh if he turned out to be the Yorkshire Ripper. Ma, I said, what alternative would I have? Even the sacred marriage bonds might snap, given that one's spouse was a mass murderer. Marriage bonds maybe, she said, but I am his Mother. Then she said would I inform on Ben, I said what else could I do and she said you could stop his pocket money. She did. Ben, I said, glaring at the stick of celery that is my son, if I hear you've murdered one *more woman*, no sixpence for you next Friday. Well, now they've arrested someone who's got a wife and a mother.

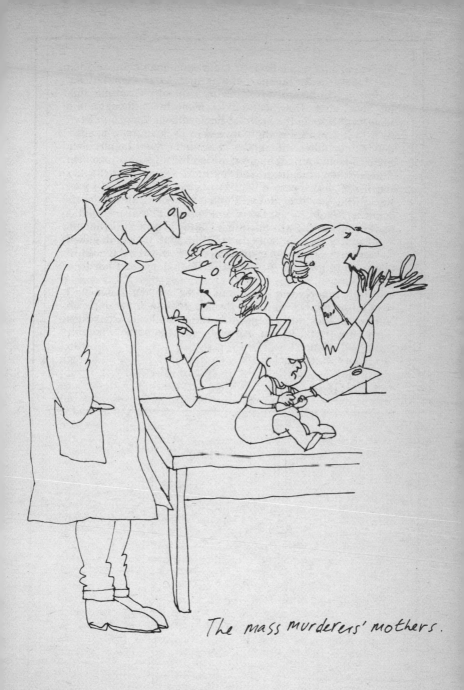

The mass murderers' mothers.

Keep your ears pinned back for the feminine connection.

Ben's friend Flanagan stayed most of the holiday. He explained that he had left home because his mother had this new boyfriend. How difficult it must be, I thought, for adolescent boys in the midst of the Oedipal Dilemma to have alien males vying for their love-object's favours. Flanagan said he couldn't stand the way his Mum bullied her boyfriends and now she had chucked them both out because of her women's meetings. You're as bad as the NFers, he told her. I can't help being a boy, can I, any more than if I was black? But you *are* black, Flanagan, I said, and Black is Beautiful. Yeah, except I'm white, he said. Flanagan's Dad is white, said Ben, so why shouldn't Flanagan choose? What am I, anyway, a racist or something? With that, they both pulled on jackets covered with swastikas and went out. At times like this, I am so grateful for the baby. Dear thing, he's hardly a boy yet at all.

You probably won't read this letter until mid-January – I read in the papers that your lot had gone to Rome to picket Nativity Scenes. My goings-on here on the home front must seem very trivial to you. Ah well, we also serve who only stand and whine.

Yours, from a hot stove,

Martha

NO DOGS
NO PRAMS

hardly a boy...

Dear Mary

So it's Arrivaderci Roma and now you're in Berlin. Lucky old you, I'm so housebound these days I have to take Kwells to get to the greengrocers. Fascinated to hear how you all burst into that German lawyer's office, debagged him and sprayed his naughty bits with blue paint. Frosted, yet. What larks, eh? Though not, I suppose, for the lawyer, who was obviously terrified you were going to perform an emergency dingalingectomy. Read out the details to Josh at breakfast and he couldn't finish his kipper. When his voice was back to normal he got very pompous about lawyers' rights to defend rapists and rapists' rights to be defended and now he knew why Justice was a woman and blind. She may be a woman, I said, burning the toast, but she is not a Sister. The law is made by the men for the men of the men and I never heard you complain about its bias against us over the last two thousand years. He stormed out in the end, saying he'd be sleeping in the spare room from now on because he wasn't having his personal plumbing redecorated by power-mad libbers. By the way, I suppose he's all right now, is he? The lawyer, I mean.

Anyway, sweet of you to say you'll get me a duty-free goodie on the boat back. In a sort of way I wouldn't say no to a bottle of scent. There, I've got it out. No, I don't want to be a sex object and I do know scent is pushy, getting up people's noses without their permission, and I don't want expensive French ooo-la-la but English Rose can't be all bad? It's natural enough, though mainly of course, on roses. There are the herby scents, too. Is one considered a sex object if one smells of coq au vin? Oh dear, that even sounds wrong – buy what you think best.

Goodness knows why I've got this yen for scent lately. Josh says women exhibit some very odd symptoms years before anything happens or, rather, doesn't happen. Our next-door neighbour's wife started laughing. It upset her husband no end, he says she's never been one for laughing before and now it's chronic. It's not as if she has much to laugh at, poor dear, what with looking after her husband's senile Mum and her boy in trouble and working nights at the Kentucky Fried. Personally, I wonder she can raise a smile. Perhaps she's read that book I picked up at the library. It said The Change was nothing to worry about because most women only got shrinking breasts, swelling hips, hot flushes and facial hair. Looking forward to being a fat red-faced flat-chested bearded lady is enough to give anyone terminal laughter.

The baby's fine, since you ask, and ever so good, even if he is a trifle permanent. I thought I'd have the babysitting problem licked, this time round, but silly me. Jane explodes if I ask her more than once a month, accuses me of chromosome exploitation, gender fascism, daughter colonization and other crimes I've never heard of, though I expect she's right. What she won't understand is that boys are so bad at it. I know I ought to persevere and prepare Ben for being a house-husband and a truly involved father in later life but should I use the baby as a teaching machine? Last time he baby-sat we couldn't find the poor wee thing for half-an-hour, though it's true he was only sitting under Ben's dismantled record player chewing a bit off Adam and the Ants. You *see*, Ben kept saying, there's nothing the *matter* with him, is there? What's all the *fuss* about? The episode hasn't done a thing for his vestigial fathering instincts, either. Now he says he'll never have kids, if everyone makes such a *fuss* about it. Bess and May at the Women's Centre have offered to come but the last time I called they were out demonstrating for 24-hour nurseries.

I'm sure all this bores you concrete, what with your very sensible decision not to have children because of men being the way they are and the world being what it is. They are and it is, I do so agree, but there he is. I don't think any of my friends have quite forgiven me for having him, especially since he's a boy, the misguided sausage. And he was premature, due to that long walk from Hyde Park Corner on the last Every Child a Wanted Child March. Is that a sort of excuse? Am enclosing snap of him. It's blurred because he has a rash and a tooth coming through and is howling.

Chalked up two bad boo-boos last week. First, we were invited by the Department to meet Josh's new boss. There were masses of people and Josh didn't introduce me to a soul, just shot off into a corner to talk shop with the pin-stripes. I felt I ought to make an effort so I said to this woman wasn't the Department a mysterious place and could she understand a word her husband told her about it? She slid off sharpish, looking like she'd just swallowed glass. Turned out she was Josh's new boss, quite good-looking in a bureaucratic way, brilliant double first, breakthrough for womankind trala. I drank rather a lot after that one.

Then, at the launderette, I got chatting with another woman, recounted the aforementioned story and said didn't she hate being asked what she did at parties and having to say she was a housewife? Quick as a flash, she turned into a militant houseperson, gave me a lecture about some women *choosing* to stay at home with the children and if women's lib wasn't about *choosing* what was it about and she couldn't stand the view that you weren't liberated until you were pinned behind a typewriter from nine to five. People like you, she said, won't be happy till you've made women robots just like men and she flounced off with her plastic bag and her three screaming kids.

Sometimes I think, Mary, that you don't quite grasp the complications we face, here at the grassroots.

Yours, covered with facial egg,

Martha

Dear Mary

Of course I understand your objection to rapists and rippers and robbers – in a word, men. But you have to understand my position. I have them in the house, Mary, three of them. Well, you can't quite count the baby yet, though he's already very demanding, wanting to be fed at inopportune moments and forcing me to drop everything and retire to the bedroom. Jane and Ben had the nerve, the other night, to ask why I couldn't breastfeed him naturally? I told them I was under the impression I was doing just that and they said they meant *in front of them.* I was shocked. Certainly *not,* I said in a Lady Bracknell voice. Then they both delivered a diatribe about Mother Nature that included references to dogs and puppies, the women of Africa and the women in Parliament who did it in front of MPs.

As coolly as I could, I pointed out to the kids that even women in Parliament tucked themselves under the Woolsack or somewhere and pretty watercolours of breastfeeding women with rosy toddlers gathered round their knees were one thing but doing it with two great yawks like them gaping down their Mother's hitherto unrevealed assets – and the possibility of Flanagan & Co. joining the merry throng – was quite another. Besides, it could wreak havoc with Ben's Oedipal Dilemma, if he had one, which I doubt. And if, Mary, you are thinking of taking their side, I would remind you that the only helpless member of God's creation you've ever fed in public was that baby guinea pig of yours and it died.

But I digress. What I meant to say was that living with men makes you realize they suffer too. This morning, Ben's face had all gone to pieces and he kept jumping suddenly, like a flea-ridden cat. Asked the matter, he said his jaw was fractured, his molars ached, his gums had gangrene, and he might quite possibly die, all because he'd spent last evening grinding his teeth at a party. But why, I said. So's to look like this, he said, clenching his teeth, sucking in his cheeks and allowing an expression of psychopathic blankness to flatten his features. But *why*, I said. At which he groaned and gibbered and smirked until I got it. He was being *High Noon* and *Gunfight at the OK Corral* and Jack Palance in anything, for the sole purpose of attracting the girls and to hell with his jawbones, his dentures, and endemic facial dystrophy. I think that's rather touching, don't you?

No, you don't. Ah well, I'll try you with a larger ethical problem – President Reagan. It took me a longish while to realize that he didn't have two heads like Zaphod Beeblebrox, one talking and the other doing the noddies. Ah *ha*, I said to myself of a sudden. So that's Mrs Reagan, the head with the hat, just like Mrs Carter before her.

Now, as you know, I'm all in favour of wives being rewarded for the unpaid labour they put in on behalf of their husbands' careers. The place is awash with the wives of vicars and doctors and diplomats and lord mayors and corporate gents (I include myself modestly in here) all flogging our guts out, gratis, for the sake of our husbands' companies, practices, parishes, towns, countries and so on. We are charming hostesses, delightful dinner-givers, caring telephone voices, judicious flatterers and soft shoulders for people to cry on so they don't wet the men's suits.

And is there a penny in it for us? There is not. Are there even thanks? Usually they go to the husband, as if he were the one who whisked up the soufflé, coped with Mrs Hoo-Ha's nasty turn and rubbed up against the boss. Though we might get a surreptitious pinch on the bottom for services rendered. I've been there, Mary.

But at the other extreme, why should the Americans get a Presidentess they never voted for? Whispering away in the President's ear without the say-so of a single ballot paper? That's power without responsibility if you like. A woman who wears red from top to toe at her husband's inauguration is not about to back out of the limelight and those who think Ron used the movies to get to be President might ask themselves if Madam Reagan isn't using the Presidency to get back into movies? Her and her bedside revolver. Who does she think is going to break in on her White House slumbers? A flying Ayatollah? That one is a bigger sabre-rattler than her Ron and it worries me. Imagine what it will do for women's image when survivors of a nuclear holocaust scuttle up from their underground caves, take a look round the ruined planet and say, 'Of course, I blame *her*.'

A friend of mine wrote from America that she never saw so many dead animals on so many women's backs as at Ron's inaugural ball – she said it looked like the biggest ecological disaster since the Raj. She mentioned this to some man standing near her and he said look at it this way, it's a triumph of biodegradability, which is more than you can say for punks and their plastic. Yes, Mary, I am aware that I possess a beaver coat but it is a very old coat and the beaver passed away yonks ago.

That's all for now except to say I do think you ought to stop harassing Shirley Williams. She is *not* the most hopeless female since Bo Peep *nor* the worst little madame since Shirley Temple and if the Chinese can suspend Mrs Mao's death sentence, surely you should follow suit? Mrs Williams has done a lot for women that I can't immediately recall and it will do no one any good to keep shouting abuse through her letter-box. At the moment she is simply a distressed gentlewoman of insecure means who needs all the sleep she can get.

Yours, from the middle of the right of centre,

Martha

President Reagan's Inaugural Ball

Dear Mary

It was lovely to see you so unexpectedly last Saturday and such a pity the visit was so short. Did you get the stain out of those super Fiorucci jeans? The trouble is, babies with nappy rash can't wear plastic pants because the ammonia in the urine gets trapped and irritates the . . . well, you don't want all the details, do you? I'm afraid Mother wasn't at her best, either. She's been over-excited ever since the Labour Conference, though why that should concern her I don't know – in Mother's political spectrum Mrs Thatcher is dripping wet. I think it was that Labour MP that set her temples throbbing again, the one who chairs the Mobilizing Committee for what she always calls the Rank and Vile but that's only her little joke and I don't honestly think she would shoot quite all the Lefties she says she'd shoot. Not dead, anyway.

And then, of course, there was Josh. It's a funny thing that when he and I are alone together, I am permitted to dig over the garden, tar the roof and clean the chimney, all without a murmur of protest from him. But you come on the scene and suddenly Josh can only just restrain his chivalrous urges out of respect for your feminism. He *would* pull out your chair but he knows you'd disapprove. He *would* uncork the wine except you'd think him an mcp. He *would* carve the roast but that might seem sexist. He *would* say how well you're looking but he doesn't want to be hit over the head with your handbag, what, what? I'm perspiring lightly, Mary, just writing this.

Repeat to yourself, over and over, that Josh is fifty. Half a century old. Women can change, whatever their age (except Mother, that is) but leave men in peace for a minute and they set like cement and spend the rest of their lives repelling the faintest whiff of a new idea as if it were a bulldozer come to hack out their foundations. Josh, let's face it, is the original unreconstructed male but he can be very sweet sometimes, in his own way. Last time I told you that, you said some people thought gorillas were cute but that's very unfair. Friends must accept friends, warts and all, particularly if they're joined to their warts in holy matrimony, as I am.

Actually, I'm sure Josh secretly admires you and is only afraid you'll subvert me and, one of these days, I'll follow you out through the front door like the Pied Piper's children, leaving him to live on boiled eggs for the rest of his life, which wouldn't be long considering what boiled eggs do for the cholesterol level. As it happens, we had the most almighty row after you'd gone (Josh says we always have the most almighty row after you've gone *and* after I've read Marilyn French *and* after I've been to my women's collective). Ask yourself *why*, I shouted at him, pourquoi, perchè, warum? Because women never know when they're well off, he said. At the time, I was down on my knees scrubbing the kitchen floor and he was spreadeagled on the sofa sipping a Scotch, though he did lift up his feet as I scrubbed by.

But enough of the squalid domestic front. Let us cast our eyes to the bracing outside world and give three cheers for another woman Prime Minister. That makes five by my count – Norway, India, Iceland, Bolivia and us. Well, Iceland is a President, not a PM, and India is more your Royalty than anything and I've got an uneasy feeling Bolivia has already hit the dust and our own Mrs. T. would be better hidden under a bushel, whatever that is.

But Norway is fair and square, a democratically elected mother of four and Labour, to boot. Odd that her husband is a leading member of the Conservative Opposition. What can it be like, to quarrel over the kitchen table *and* the front benches? or perhaps Norwegians, up to their knees in permafrost, can maintain a matrimonial *sang froid* unknown to the warm-blooded, volatile English.

Not that I think it's done our Cause much good, some of the women who've made the Top Job. Men have managed to live under male monsters – Hitler, Stalin, Caligula, Peter the Great, Attila the Hun – without drawing any derogatory conclusions about their own sex but let a woman add 2p to the cost of false teeth and all anti-feminist hell breaks loose. On the other hand, Josh voted for Mrs T. and still thinks this makes him an honorary founder member of the Women's Movement. Whenever I register an egalitarian complaint he says he voted for a woman Prime Minister didn't he, so how can anyone accuse him of being against women's liberation?

Two jokes that are making the school rounds now, just to keep you in touch with an adolescent world you will never, the Goddess willing, know at first hand: what did Elvis Presley get for Christmas? Answer, John Lennon. And what do Paul McCartney and John Lennon have in common? Answer, Wings. Well, at least they're non-sexist. A Chinese friend who came from Hong Kong last week adds an inscrutable Chinese quip. She says whenever the Chinese criticize the Gang of Four, they hold up five fingers, thus indicating the silent presence of Mr Mao among their souvenirs. She maintains that if Jiang Qing were to appear on Peking pavements, in two seconds there wouldn't be a shred of her left unlynched. Oh dear.

How, I often worry, are we going to prevent these token women turning the tide against us for good? And talking of token women, I've spend the last two days getting Josh's wardrobe washed and ironed for his trip next week to Brussels for the Department. He's accompanying his new boss who is, if you remember, this summa cum laude trollop who thinks I am just a Wife and will soon be sending me memos in triplicate on where to buy Josh's ties. Josh is in a state of most unJoshlike nerves. Is it permitted for Sisters to burst into other Sisters' offices and hit them hard across their lipsticked chops?

Yours, with a fist clenched,

Martha

Dear Mary

Well, well. What a lot of plots are being hatched chez vous. Is your friend Mo the one with the purple scalp? Fancy her starting a new Party and already having the support of every squatter on her block. 'Women Against Everything Against Women!' is certainly a very comprehensive name but had you thought that its initials make WAEAW, which isn't the easiest acronym I've ever heard. A cry for help, really. Is that what Mo had in mind?

Obviously, all real feminists must be disillusioned with the three existing parties – four, probably, by the time you read this. As you say, all of them are male, never mind what female fairy they've stuck on the top of the tree. What with the closet Right and the butch Left and the spayed Centre, where do women come in?

The Right do their male-bonding (which is to say female-unbonding) in prep schools, public schools and ghastly clubs and call themselves Monetarists, which is just a Tory word for Muggers; they don't actually hit women over the head and snatch our handbags, they just make sure no money gets into the handbags in the first place.

The Left pinch your bottom while you make the tea, propose snide anti-women motions at trade union meetings (like the one you sent me about 'pets' being their owners' responsibility, when they meant 'children') and shout 'take it off' at strippers in their working men's clubs.

As for the Liberal Democratic Council for Being Jolly D. to Everybody, we know they have no visible means of support and will therefore instantly require all female members to spend their entire time making jam and organizing jumble sales. At most we can only expect a prize for the woman who knits the best party policy without using a pattern.

I expect you're right when you say Foot and Benn the Flowerpot Men aren't really interested in women's equality or they'd get their pronouns sorted out but it is unkind of you to add that Foot is, anyway, overdue for his meeting with the Great Chiropodist in the Sky.

So when I read about your idea, I thought it was brill, as Ben would say. Better than Mo's, in the long run. A Feminist Tendency that infiltrates the Tories as sleepers (ho ho) and then erupts, at designated times, against particularly repulsive policies. I've always felt that this kind of subversion would be far more effective than constantly scratching away at those who believe more or less as you do – people take more notice of you if you've got a sterling anti-Them pedigree and then suddenly come down on Their side.

Is it possible that there are men doing it at this very moment? Viz Very-Right-Wing Tory John Gorst proclaiming that he's got his reservations about telephone-tapping? Or the Right-Wing MPs against Murdoch? Don't you feel an awful temptation to forgive them all their past sins and love them? Whereas boring old Labour MPs who've been against everything since Runnymede merely make you yawn? Well, not you, perhaps. Me.

The only flaw in your idea that I can see is that infiltration is a slow business and you won't have that much time if the Duke of Edinburgh has his way. Should I start a campaign naming him as HRH Nuclear Waste personified? Next thing we know, he'll be blasting the grouse off Scottish moors with a Cruise missile. Personally, I don't believe he'd even qualify as a Third-Class British citizen unless the Tories have in mind a special loophole for itinerant Royals.

And I bet he's got a nuclear shelter built under Buck House where the Royals can breed through 5,000 years of radiation half-life. But with them, who would notice?

Anyway, count me in as a founder member of the Feminist Tendency and the WAEAW, but *don't tell Josh*. It's Department policy that none of its staff 'or their wives' should be members of any political party. A detached overview, says Josh, must be seen to be held. Rather than actually held, he means, since no one in the Department, including friend husband, would dream of voting anything but Tory.

Chez moi, unlike toi, all is stasis. Josh left yesterday, rising like a pin-striped waistcoated Phoenix from the ashes of his home to fly Sandy or Debbie or Whoever to Brussels. It transpires that his boss lives not far away, so she collected him in her white Porsche 924 de luxe, sun roof, tinted glass, at 8 am. I'd been packing his suitcase since seven and was still in my dressing-gown so I couldn't emerge to meet her, like Mr Rochester's wife. Josh just shouted goodbye up the stairs, doubtless leaving Ms Boss with a cockle-warming impression of wifely sluttishness and neglect.

I peered out of the bedroom window and saw her wearing, I swear, a Jean Muir original, with hair so sprayed it didn't budge in the force nine gale. And get this, Josh opened the car door for her. That could have been me in there, Mary, if I hadn't sacrificed everything for love.

And what has love got me? A Marks and Sparks candlewick unoriginal and a fortnight's family camping in France. Men, I feel, are like wine – before buying, a real connoisseur takes a small sip and spits them out. If only I could spit Josh far enough away that he would have to look back and see me as more than a bunch of electricity bills chewed to the shape of a woman. It was St. Valentine's Day last Saturday, but all I got was a card from a plumber, saying he'd fix my pipes.

Yours, with a leaking heart,

Martha

25 February

Dear Mary

I've got an old bone to pick with you. No, I'd better re-word that. I should like to discuss my spouse with you, one Josh. Look, when you moan to me about some hitch in one of your campaigns or an ideological spat or something, do I ever write back and just say, flatly, give it up then? I do not. I scratch about in the dim folds of my grey matter in order to come up with some constructive solution or subtle circumnavigation. I do not blow even metaphorical raspberries. But when I complain to you about Josh, you more or less imply that if I haven't dumped, executed or otherwise dispatched him by return of post I will be drummed out of the women's movement and forcibly enrolled in my local chapter of the Mother's Union. This is unhelpful.

Why is it that you're perfectly happy battling men in the abstract – the patriarchal society, the male ethos, the masculine principle blah blah – and say you're a champion of Womankind, yet if one woman complains about one man you don't want to know? I've noticed that about some feminists. They'll devote their lives to the struggle of the sexes but any individual manifestation of that struggle and they go into spasms of boredom and contempt. Unless, of course, the man is a really big concrete nasty, a rapist or a batterer of his wife, in which case she'll get all the support she can use.

But the sort of problems I have, representing as they do ordinary women's lives in the patriarchal society, like packing Josh's suitcase and washing his socks and not flying anywhere because of the baby, dry up even your crocodile tears. The ties between a man and a woman, Mary, are a mite too complex to be completely solved by shouting *stuff* 'im. There's sex for a start and I don't fancy women, even if that is the result of masculine conditioning, like Adrienne Rich says. I'm too old to get de-conditioned now. Besides, how many women are going to get turned on by me in my candlewick dressing-gown, tastefully spotted by the baby's second thoughts? With all the conditioning on their side, I don't notice men battering down my door for the chance to possess my middle-aged spread, never mind two delinquent teenagers and a blotchy sort of baby, and I haven't had the glad-eye from a woman since I was Miss Shaw's favourite goal-keeper back in the Upper Fifth. I'm not sure they make 'em like Miss Shaw any more.

The truth is, Mary, that many women defect or never get involved with feminism in the first place because they see all too clearly that Achilles is their Heel and they can't afford to start from there, especially if they've already given birth to little Achilleses. Do try thinking of me as, say, a subsistence tenant farmer and Josh as the wicked landowner. You'd hardly give the tenant farmer a ticking-off for not having upped stakes, would you? Sometimes I'd *like* to walk out but what's the point of disappearing into a feminist sunset hand in hand with nothing?

Depressing, isn't it, that the only triumph for women last week was Princess Anne winning over Nelson Mandela and Jack Jones as Chancellor of London University? Still, it must be a majority of men that put her there and I imagine men suffer more from Mummy dreams about the Royal ladies than we do. It made me feel Princess Anne was only too right when she said higher education was an over-rated pastime. If it gets her into office over a man who's spent 20 years in prison for fighting injustice, it certainly is. I don't think I'll take that Open University course, after all. It might give me weak knees, a symptom of what we doctors call the Curtseying Syndrome.

By the way, when I said I'd help your friend Mo's 'Women Against Everything Against Women" party, I didn't mean I was yearning to spend the next fortnight licking envelopes. Mo's envelopes have a particularly disgusting taste and will probably pollute my maternal milk and poison the baby. Why can't Mo's male supporters lick them for a change and give us women the space to go power mad? Tell her I'll do this lot now they're here but one of the Things Against Women is definitely envelope-licking. Mixed bag of names she's come up with, hasn't she? Mrs Whitehouse only represents Women Against, Mrs Kennedy seems a trifle far-flung, I'm sure Leila Khaled gives all her money to the Golan Heights Home for Retired Hi-jackers and I think Anais Nin is dead.

You don't think Mo had anything to do with that lot who fired on the Greek Patriarch last week, do you? She did mention, in her note with the envelopes, that she was going to be in the Middle East shortly. Could the title 'Patriarch' have

overly inflamed her? I hope not. As a woman and mother of three I cannot condone violence, even against Patriarchs wearing funny hats and if Mo is, by any chance, fancying herself as the Baader-Meinhof of Sebastopol Terrace, I'm afraid I shall have no option but to withdraw my spit from her envelopes.

Meanwhile, back at the ranch, Ben has acquired four white mice. I was rather chuffed when I heard him call one of them Goethe. There are literary hopes for that boy I thought, until I realised he was only saying Gertie. Apparently, they're all Gerties, so they won't breed, though how Ben can tell I don't know. From their expressions, he says. I suppose they all look itsy-bitsy cute, said Jane crossly. No, just dumb, said Ben. They broke Josh's spare specs, fighting, *after that*.

I'd just had a phone call from Josh in Brussels. He said he was speaking from the office but, if so, they've just hired a 10-piece band on the ratepayers' money. He wanted to remind me to write to the Gas Board. It's wonderful to know I'm in his thoughts, even when he's over the water. I bet that Ms Boss of his with the sticky hair approves of open-ended marriages. I bet you do too. Even I might, if the open-end revealed anything more alluring than our eighty-year-old postman.

Yours, in a state of non-specific arousal,

Martha

Dear Mary

This week I've been slogging through a housewife's hell. Monday, the baby decided to recapture its youth and began waking at 6 am again, demanding milk, women and song. Ben, on the other hand, off for half-term, never appeared before noon. Pretty soon the household had split into different time zones – him having breakfast Down Under, me having a midnight snack in the Old Country. Then the fridge flipped its lid and started making ice like it had just bought shares in John Curry.

Twenty phone calls later I raised a sleeping beauty in the repair department who said she'd send a man but couldn't promise an a.m. or a p.m. You mean to say, I said, that I have to stay chained *chez moi* from nine to five to suit the whims of your repairman? If Doctor Finlay could make appointments, why can't you? Just wait, I said. One of these days it'll be you at home going bonkers, Miss Brook Street Bureau, and then you'll be sorry you didn't show solidarity with your female customers. Pardon? she said. I could *hear* her filing her nails.

So all day Tuesday I stayed in but I did, once, go to the loo. I have this weak bladder. When I got downstairs again, there was the card on the doormat. 'Your repairman called but could not get an answer.' Printed, it was, all ready for him to stuff, quick as a flash, through the letterbox and run off, chortling. Back on the phone to sleeping beauty, confined to barracks another whole day and the repairman finally cometh, regardeth the fridge and tutteth. Tut tut, he says. Nasty, that. Haven't got the tools in the van for *that*. Oh yes? I said. Has this fridge broken down in ways no fridge has ever broken down before? Is this a First for Fridgedom? A breakthrough for Fridgekind? Has Dutch Elm disease struck again, is there dry rot in its private parts? The repairman's eyes flicked from side to side, looking – I dare say – for the gents in white and I wouldn't have said no to a short interval in the funny farm myself.

I'm on the phone again, this time to some man called a

Customer Liaison Officer. That's a very strange story, madam, he says, very strange. Strange to you, maybe, I shout, but deeply familiar to me, mate, and I'll bet it's familiar to your wife, too. Shall I tell you why we never see appliances break down on Coronation Street or Crossroads or even Soap? No, madam, he says. Because you can't keep an audience on the edge of their seats by showing them women on the edge of their seats, waiting for repairmen. You can have women kissing the lodger or winning the pools or linging alongaMax but you can't have them sitting there twiddling their thumbs, waiting for repairmen. That isn't what is called good telly, but that's what half of England's wives are doing half of the time in what is called real life.

Sometimes, Mary, I think, stuff a liberated sex life and the Sexual Opportunities Bill. What we housewives want is the nitty gritty. In Mexico they've just permitted women to drink in men's bars but the women can't because Mexican barmen won't put in women's loos and a world traveller like you should know what tequila does to the system. Withholding loos is the way they always keep women out of where they want in. Storm any barricade and behind it there's the inevitable man with his hands up saying back, girls, no loo. So what we need is Super Repairwoman. At the clap of a housewife's hands, she'd zoom in with her kit and give the breath of life to any appliance. At another clap she'd streak across the sky with her portable Elsan, to the cheers of feminists everywhere. Here comes the Germaine Greer of the S-Bend, we'd yell. Hurrah!

Dreams, dreams. Meanwhile, Ben's been driving me mad fiddling with things. Yesterday, he wandered into my bedroom and absent-mindedly stuck a No Nukes badge in Latin I'd been saving for the car slap on the side of my walnut cupboard. His huge hands just went fiddle fiddle all by themselves and there it was, unpeeloffable. I threatened to go into his room and do something terrible to it, for revenge, and Jane said like what, Ma? Clean it? Now I can't find the Optrex that was in my bedroom and I know Ben's nicked it. Can you get high, sniffing Optrex?

Referring to yours of the ult. (yes, I know I'm being really self-centred this week) I can't agree that the plighting of the Royal troth removes the last excuse for any nubile girl in the Western hemisphere to say no. Nubile Jane, for instance, is so blank about royalty in general that when our neighbour mentioned the Prince of Wales' engagement she thought he was on about a gig at the local pub. And Jane *always* says no to men, anyway. *Yuk no* and *ugh no* and *aargh no*. Sometimes I worry about that girl. But at least we've seen the last of those caveman articles about Lady This and Princess von That not being suitable on account of their purple pasts. Marvellous, isn't it, that it's perfectly OK for anyone in skirts to be profoundly conversant with Prince C's nocturnal habits but too hideous to contemplate a male who's even *swum* over the future Q of E and lived to tattle-tale. And they say women are gossips?

Josh's secretary rang just now to pass on his home thoughts from abroad. Back at the weekend, bringing Ms Boss for a bite, would I get food in and please remember, this time, have ice ready for drinkies. Ice? The way that fridge is acting, I'll soon be engulfed in a glacial tide like the last of the dinosaurs, my youth preserved forever to mock Josh's greying hairs.

Yours, on the rocks,

Martha

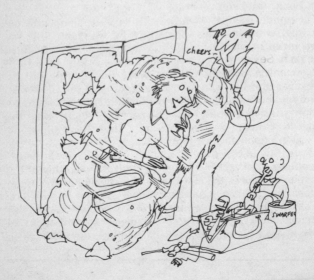

Dear Mary

How my heart raced when I read your last letter and learnt that your Women's Sub-Orgasmic Therapy Group has been discussing little me. Or rather, as you most discreetly put it, 'my type'. Such a relief you all concluded that 'my type' is not really neurotic *as such* but is merely 'an organism appropriately adapted to a restricted environment like a crossopterygian fish'. Well, ta ever so, Sisters. A man once told me his wife never cooked *as such* and another man confided that he didn't have sex *as such*. I couldn't bring myself to ask as such *what* in case the answer was too boggly but I do know I'm not at all like a crossopwhatsit fish, even as such.

Personally, since you're not asking, I think people who keep talking to cushions, as you say your group does, are already well on the road to the bin and no as such about it. And I'd be glad if you'd inform the next cushion you converse with that this particular organism will shortly leave its restricted environment and hit them all over the head with its appropriately adapted handbag unless they stop discussing it instanter. As for you, be warned. One of these days I may be forced to telephone the News of the Screws and reveal to a stunned public that behind Smash Video-Porn and Vegans Against Sexism and Lesbians for the Whale and Women Pavement Artists' Workshop and Wages Due Very Small Grannies in Hair Nets there is only you and Mo squatting on overdue library books at Sebastopol Terrace with an old Imperial you ripped-off back stage, the night you raided the Miss World contest. So watch it.

My friend in America sent me this really depressing article, all about how the whole country is awash with wonderfully warm, highly educated, deeply brilliant and purposefully independent women who come home from their executive jobs and spend the nights sobbing in their lonely beds because they can't find a single man who isn't either gay or being mobbed on all sides by hundreds of other wonderfully warm, highly educated etcetera women hungry for their annual quickie. At least I think the writer meant quickie but you never know with Americans – one came into the pub the other day and asked for a mushroom quickie, which was the cute way he pronounced quiche.

And the article went on that when these men do decide to marry, they 'marry down,' which means they get themselves hitched to dumb blondes well below them on the evolutionary ladder, which must take some doing. Of course, that's a typical mcp ploy, making sure you're top dog by picking a pussy cat of very few brains with whom to exchange vows of eternal domination-submission, but we have to remember that though American men are God's gift to no one, all those warm, wonderful women are also American. That means most of them spend most of their time verifying their perceptualizations, relating to their authentic selves, demanding positive ego-reinforcement, diagnosing their Irritable Bowel Syndrome (IBS), detailing their Pre-Menstrual Tension (PMT) and then telling everyone to have a good day. No wonder the sexes are drifting apart. Never mind. If things go on this way, Americans will shortly stop producing little Americans, the whole nation will vanish from the earth and we can all breathe a sigh of relief.

And another thing, Mary, before we bury the Gestalt hatchet. I'm sure it's very nice and unselfish of you to say you're working on your feelings with the aim of becoming a truly caring and accessible friend but, to tell you the honest truth, I prefer the old uncaring fairly inaccessible you I know and love. OK? As for me, I have been taking lessons from old Mother Nature who is all around me, especially in Ben's room. There, amongst the luxuriant flora and fauna – curls of dry orange peel, banana skins, stale jam crusts, half bottles of festering milk and cups containing tea leaves half as old as time – two of God's little creatures live and have their being. Ben won them three years ago on Hampstead Heath and brought them home, two goldfish in a plastic bag. Ever since, they have swum round and round in a green and slimy bowl, hardly ever cleaned, hardly ever fed. I have threatened to call in the Hunt Saboteurs to spray lemon in his eyes, I have vowed that the Animal Liberation Front will vivisect him in his bed but all to no avail. Yet do the wretched fish protest? They do not. His friends' goldfish, treated properly, have all given up their little goldfish souls a long time ago. His flourish. Their scales gleam, their fins waggle, they are clearly in the pink.

Same applies to the Gerties, Ben's white mice. Sunk in

Stygian gloom, their only pals the gaping goldfish, nothing to do all day but hide their heads in straw and they're happy as clams and what, for heaven's sake, have clams to be happy about? Plants are the same. Leave them in draughts over radiators, their earth as dry as Arizona and what do they do? Put out shy little shoots and coy buds. Start to care, bustle around them, give them doses of plant food, chat to them and they reward you by turning brown and passing away.

There's a lesson there for us all, Mary, and especially for me. Neglect is Good. Care kills. And that is my new life plan for Josh. He didn't come home at the weekend after all. No sooner had I transferred the contents of Sainsburys to my pantry and the fridge had produced enough ice to sink the *Titanic* than I got his cable. Can only make it back Thursday, bringing Irene. So Ms Boss is now Irene, is she? Well, this is my new scenario. Hullo Irene. Hullo Josh. Have some green slime? A little stale fishmeal? I'm off to beddy-byes. Goodnight Irene.

Yours, from a whole new space,

Martha

A Whole New Space

Dear Mary

I knew I'd get the fall-out from your new caring self. So I was mean about America, was I? What do you think that'll do? Sink our Special Relationship in mid-Atlantic? Blow the San Andreas Fault? Mary, I'm just a slightly overweight London housewife writing to a friend and I know you're into cosmic responsibility but this is ridiculous. As for what I said about the women, well, I had one of my heads at the time. I do realize that Sisters in their little nests should agree and that being warm, wonderful and deeply human isn't a capital crime.

It's just that American women make me feel inferior and superior at the same time and that's an uneasy mix. How can they whip up batches of brownies while being Executive Directors of Computer Software (Far East) Inc. while writing world best-sellers while raising four Junior Citizens on fluoride toothpaste and shots of vitamin B12 when I come over a bit queer just getting the milk bottles in from the doorstep? Nevertheless, they are also silly. I can't explain how, they just are.

And so will you be if you insist on training yourself in Caring. You've got it wrong Mary. Women should care a bit less so that men are made to care a bit more. Daily, I conduct my own one-woman in-home classes. Martha, I say to myself, today you will not care that the floor needs scrubbing, the sink is blocked and we're down to two fish fingers. You will not care that the roses are unpruned and the cats unwormed. You will ignore Ben demanding who's pinched his Biology Project, Jane moaning about how boring everything is and Mother just moaning. Don't care was made to care, my father used to say, but he meant me, not him.

Before my new leaf turned, I worried about everything. Starving Ethiopians, gulls in oil slicks, mugged old ladies, badgers, apartheid, Sri Lankan workers on tea plantations and the bits that fall off Suffolk villages when juggernauts drive by. You name it, I've cared about it. My cheeks have fallen in, my teeth are falling out, I've got white flecks on my nails and a twitchy sciatic nerve and still Ethiopians starve, gulls get oiled and bits fall off Suffolk villages. Whereas Josh, who only cares about the MLR and the state of his shirts, blooms.

Yes, Josh has finally returned. He and Ms Boss – or Irene, as I am now instructed to call her – zoomed back from Brussels on Thursday. They were high on travel, I was low on home sweet home. Irene must be at least my age but then so am I, so that's no advantage and as far as coiffures go, I'm still cantering up to the starting post. Josh remarked on how small and dark the kitchen looked, Irene said everything was delightful. Delightful home, delightful baby, delightful to meet delightful me. She said Ben was delightful too, and even I, who gave him birth, know that delightful he isn't.

I stuck three frozen pizzas in the oven and she said how delightful home cooking was, after hotels. When I said I could do with some hotel cooking myself, she gave me such an understanding chuckle, put her hand over mine and told me she knew I didn't mean that because home cooking and motherhood was the most rewarding career of all. What conversational exchange is left after that? Tisn't, tis, tisn't, tis? I wanted to say why waste your time then, rushing off to foreign parts with other people's husbands and getting four million pounds a year, if boiling nappies is your heart's desire, but Josh gave me one of his looks.

All through the meal they both chatted merrily on about macroeconomics and private equity investments and people called names like Hoofy van Winkle and Jay Bee. Mind you, Irene was most polite. She kept leaning over to include me. Hoofy, she'd say, is the MD of IBD International. Had I noticed, she'd say, the pre-Budget 5 per cent over base rate and oh and yes and would you believe it, I'd say. What stick do I have, Mary? All I hear about is the 10 per cent rise in brassicas and that's only the price of cabbages in fancy dress. If home-making is so deeply rewarding, how come no women who aren't doing it want to hear about it. You don't, do you? I just keep telling you because it's good for you.

I mean, take two of my aunties. Mother rang about them last week. So sad about Aunt May, she said. Always so neat, lived for the children and Uncle John. Now she's gone peculiar. Came to see Mother, stared at her for a while, said 'I want my tea', stuffed herself with scones and cake, said 'I want to go now,' and went; waddled off, says Mother, fat as a house, her hair all over the place. As for Aunt Myrtle, she spends all her waking hours packing. She packs, Uncle Eddie

Another Whole New Space

unpacks, she packs, Uncle Eddie unpacks. Mother puts on her compassionate voice and says it's senile dementia and they ought to be put in homes.

I say it's getting what you want at last, or trying.

Those two old ladies have looked after other people all their lives and now that they're looking after themselves, they're instantly called dotty and locked up. I said to Josh, the night he came back, would he put me in a home if I ate cake all day and packed, like Aunties May and Myrtle and he said (compassionately) that he supposed he'd have to. Still, he'd brought me a very pretty nightie edged with Brussels lace and we retired to have a good time in it. We might have done, if Ben hadn't knocked on the bedroom door in the middle, asking could he have £3 for an all-night movie and where were his Converse All-Stars and did I know the baby was crying? Good idea, your Sub-Orgasmic Group, Mary, but what happens once you are orgasmic? Ben is what happens. I'm sure he's already had sex himself but clearly it's never crossed his mind that Josh and I have too or why would he rattle the door and shout Mum, it's *locked*, in an informative sort of voice. Can he still think step-fathers are just step-*fathers*?

Which reminds me, I got a letter from Ben's father yesterday. He says he's writing a book entitled *The Flasher's Guide to Feminism*, but more of that in my next.

Yours, frustrated,

Martha

Dear Mary

Ask yourself this. If the Pill is a conspiracy against women, as you insist, who's conspiring with whom for whose benefit? I know it has nasty side effects but what doesn't? My life is filled with nasty side effects – blocked drains, cat's hairs on the sofa, pains around the heart. Come to that, the whole human race may be a side effect of some galactic spray for eradicating bugs on Betelgeuse Two. You complain the Pill is making you fat but pregnancy, Mary, is not an on-going slimming situation.

I am older and sadder than you and the things I've had to do with tubes of jelly in my time still return to haunt me on moonless nights. In those days, the sexual urge meant retiring to the bathroom with your armoury and emerging hours later, all precautions taken and all urges gone, in you and your partner, who was already snoring. And being forced to fiddle about like that before your loved one had even raised an eyebrow made you feel peculiarly pushy – the rude version of taking your harp to the party and having nobody ask you to play.

The Pill being only for women is a bore but what is the alternative? Suppose they'd invented a male-only Pill – then we'd really be in the conspiracy business. Imagine having to ask a man are you, you know, on it, and then, too late, finding out he wasn't on it and he'd dropped you in it. What would you say then? Naughty boy? Of course it's unfair, swallowing something that keeps your body in permanent hormonal upheaval but trusting men to see you all right would simply mean turning false pregnancies, abracadabra, into the real thing. On that principle, I'd have thirteen kids by now and feminism wouldn't be a twinkle in anyone's eye.

Anyway, the really crucial information you've coyly withheld is – why are you taking the Pill all of a sudden? I thought the only male you ever received, so to speak, was the bloke from the Electricity. Can you have experienced true love at last, crammed cheek to cheek with a Council Official in a cupboard under the stairs? But you don't go in for high-tech at Sebastopol Terrace, do you? I reckon it's all to do with your friend Mo being away. If she were there, she wouldn't let you take a wine gum, never mind a man-made, multinational, pharmaceutical con-trick like the Pill.

By the way, where on earth *is* Mo and why? I got a card from her last week. It showed a scrubby sort of desert being pecked at by some large and sinister black birds, the stamp was obliterated by squiggly marks and all it said, in those scratchy red ink capitals Mo uses when she's about to flip her lid, was: 'We Know DisGracefully LiTTle abouT the KUrds; in Pan-ARabiC SisterHood, Mo.' Well, as it happens, I do know disgracefully little about the Kurds and I'll bet they know disgracefully little about me. D'you think she's using some kind of code? All that leaps to mind in the way of *double-entendres* is a dreary kind of cheese. Is she a prisoner in a factory farm? Please reveal all in your next or I shall have to table a question in the House.

After a refreshing bout of post-travel togetherness, Josh has lapsed back into male separatism and is presently slumped in front of the telly. Ludovic Kennedy has just said Patrick Moore will introduce Uranus and Josh has just said 'not mine, he won't.' But mostly he's been working late at the office. The awesome possibility occurs that the whole feminist struggle has only achieved the kind of role reversal that means male Secretaries have affairs with their female bosses. If so, I shall shortly collapse, stabbed to the heart with a cliché. They say power is an aphrodisiac – does that go for powerful women, too? Perhaps, after hours, Irene goes on the town arm-in-arm with Mrs T, both of them buying drinks all round, ogling young men in G-strings and telling Josh and Denis to stop sulking or they won't take them out any more. We may soon read all about it in the gutter press and when Josh appears, hands over face, trousers down, in a smeary snapshot on the front page, I shall fold my tent and stomp away. Again.

I told you Ben and Jane's father (Tom, if you remember that far back) wrote last week, first letter in a year, but I didn't tell you what he said. What he said was, he hoped I wasn't turning *his* son into a Mother's boy. That, after seeing *his* son exactly three times in eight years and never giving me a brass aduki bean towards his upbringing. Pause for my apoplectic fit. Then he asked for money, a float – as he put it – while he writes *The Flasher's Guide to Feminism* which, he assures me, will be a wild best-seller and enable him to shower me and *his* offspring with gold. The whole idea is

Reading Mo's card

repulsive and typical of my macho ex. I told Josh how revolting I found it. Josh said yes indeedy, and looked thoughtful.

Well, Mary my love, tomorrow we shall a have little stranger among us, a brand-new baby political Party. I must say, the run-up has been fascinating, rather like being told the facts of life for the first time. The other Parties have been around so long I never liked to ask how they got there in case the answer was rude. Now I feel I've been watching an educational documentary called Where Did I Come From? Are you sitting comfortably, kiddies? Then I'll begin.

First, we have a Mummy-lady and a Daddy-man. They like each other so they ask all their friends if they should get married and their friends say yes and so they do, with the Bride wearing something old, something new, a lot borrowed and most of it Blue. Oh what lovely telegrams and prezzies they get! Then they rent a little house, open a joint bank account and soon they're sending their friends cards saying they're expecting. Everyone is very excited and very supportive of the Mummy-lady because she has attacks of quite bad heartburn, which often happens when ladies are expecting. But at last, her ordeal is over, she's come out of Labour and there they are, the proud parents of a tiny, wrinkled SDP. Aaah.

Yours, winking back a tear,

Martha

Dear Mary

Describing the new man in your life to me, your bosomy chum, as 'this bloke in the next-door squat with a double-barrel name' hardly scales the Heights of Wuthering but is, nevertheless, revealing. You are ashamed of him, Mary, and so you should be, unless he's under sixteen, in which case you should be ashamed of yourself. Any man who hasn't lost his hyphen after that age is telling the world something that I, for one, don't wish to know. People called Pyddlington-Potty or whatever have no right to inhabit squats because it is a well-known fact that they always have Pyddlington-Potty relatives in large country houses where they could squat in the east wing without anyone ever noticing, instead of taking away valuable squatting room from those who need it. I dare say he goes down to Potty Hall at weekends and makes the house party scream with his stories of one's life in one's squat. Thank heavens for the Pill, then. Otherwise you'd soon be adding to the sum of Pyddlington-Pottys and one of the many things this country doesn't need is more of them.

You'll be telling me next that he's just down from Oxford, where he had one long hoot being unutterably silly in the Piers Gaveston Society or whatever that club is called where they all camp about pretending to be Evelyn Waugh. Even E. Waugh, by all accounts, tried not to be E. Waugh all the time. Really, I despair of women. The more liberated and independent we fancy ourselves, the more we dredge up our atavistic talent for flattening ourselves under the boots of moral idiots. At this very moment half my lovely women friends are squabbling like a pack of starlings over a drunken male named, believe it or not, Studs, who calls them all chicks and acts as if he had a bit-part in a 1930s B-movie. He wears a Jimmy Cagney hat and we all know Cagney only liked women if they were Mothers and then only if they were Irish Mothers and then only if they were his Irish Mother.

I shall have to make sure Jane doesn't hear about your passing weakness – you know how she admires you. Whenever she narrows her eyes at Josh, she's thinking Mary wouldn't put up with him, unlike her doormat Mum, though of course she doesn't know what she's been spared by not being better acquainted with her own father, Tom, the John Wayne of Mousehole.

My daughter is a sore trial to me at times, especially now that she's off from the LSE. She looms about looking as grim as Bernadette MacAliskey and at least Bernadette has a lot to look grim about. Just yesterday I was glooming on about all these newspapers being bought up by Diggers and Tinies and so on, trying to explain to Jane about millionaires and monopolies and the Freedom of the Press. All she does is shrug and say she couldn't give a tinker's because whoever buys them will still fill every page with articles calculated to bore her rigid. They'll keep on blathering about the War, for a start. Any War. Then they'll dig up a fifth diary about what one Cabinet Minister said to another Cabinet Minister before she was born. Then they'll discover sixteen million more letters in an old picnic hamper from a Woolf to a Bell, then they'll drivel on about ten crashing bores at Oxbridge in 1920 and then when she, Jane, is already catatonic, they'll start another ninety-part series on the memoirs of Mugg.

Who is Mugg, she says, making horrible faces. What on earth did he do? I think, I said with some dignity, he was editor of Punch once. Oh, says Jane. I see, says Jane. That accounts for it, says Jane, falling on the floor and writhing about in a very irritating fashion. Your stepfather admires him, I informed her, Josh frequently says Mr Muggeridge is the quintessential Man of his Time. Then give me Page Three any day, says Jane and flounces out, doing some rather vulgar body language as she goes.

Of course, that's par for Jane's present course. Nothing pleases her, Mugg included. She doesn't like men, she doesn't like children, she doesn't even like puppies. A neighbour's dog just had six of the sweetest little roly-poly things but Jane just said 'Yuk' when she saw them and announced that they gave her the creeps. She went babysitting last week to earn herself some pin-money and came back swearing she wouldn't go any more because they had this silly baby who argued all the time. How can a three-month-old argue?

Then I went out for the first time in months and bought myself a gorgeous pair of sort of bronze-coloured high-heel shoes and showed them to Jane. She practically had a convulsion on the spot, yukking and ughing till I almost hoped she'd choke. Call yourself liberated, she kept saying, and you're going to walk about propped up on top of those?

Teetering around like some ancient geisha girl with bound feet?

I said don't be so rude and then she got all serious and said no, really how could I? Didn't I realize that high heels were a male plot to make women look like silly twits, unable even to walk with any efficiency? Dear Josh came in just then and said the shoes were lovely and made my ankles look delectably fragile. He actually whistled at me as I paraded about.

I could hear Jane making sickey noises all the way up the stairs. Josh said take no notice and gave me a delicious kiss, first one for quite a while. Then he said he'd decided to give Tom the money he wanted to write *The Flasher's Guide to Feminism*. So I followed Jane up the stairs, making sickey noises, and twisted my ankle on the landing, due to the high-heel shoes.

Yours, in a no-win situation,

Martha

Dear Mary

No letter on my doormat this week. Either you and Pyddlington-Potty have sunk for good and all into your waterbed, leaving naught but plastic beakers and a faint oil slick to mark the final submergence or you're angry with me or both. Perhaps Potty has abandoned you for a girl with gold bits in her Gucci shoes called Cynthia Yeovil-Orne (pronounced Yawn) and you're shut in the broom cupboard, agrophobic with grief. I wish you had a telephone. It's an awfully useful device, you know. We could say hullo and guess who and you could shout the line is bad and all manner of interesting things. Without it, I worry about you. Who would look after you if you're ill? True, Josh only notices I'm laid low by the milk bottles piling up outside but you haven't anyone in the house, unless Mo has returned from desert parts.

Actually, I imagine you're quite all right, just off me for the moment because of my remarks about P-P having a name like P-P. Forgive me. I was intolerant, impolite and class-ridden. People cannot help what they are called. After all, Mr Benn was born hyphenated and though he's been doing his best to lose it ever since, half England still distrusts him because he once had it and the other half because he's dropped it. If you like Pyddlington-Potty, then so do I and I expect his real names are something perfectly acceptable like . . . er . . . Well, never mind. I'll tell you a gruesome secret about me and then we'll be quits. I still call my Mother Mummy. Yes, I know that's utterly pathetic. A shrink I went to when I was in that fearful state of indecision about whether to leave Tom for Josh (the shrink said don't) informed me that women who call their Mothers Mummy suffer from unresolved identity conflicts. He spent the whole hour going on about breast fixations and nipple substitutes and oral infantilism and all the time he was sucking away on this really giant pipe, slurp, slurp. Amazing.

I explained to him that I call Mother Mummy so as not to hurt her feelings but, apparently, not wanting to hurt one's

Luring back the Sun God

Mother's feelings is a serious psychic perversion. What am I supposed to do to signify maternal liberation, put the poor old bag through the Magimix? Speaking as a Mother myself (called Mum by Ben and Martha by Jane) I'd be only too glad to have my feelings spared but, as all good shrinks know, we Mothers devote our entire lives to deforming and stunting our offspring until such time as one of them smacks us round the chops and steams off into the sunset, adult at last. How unfair it all is. When I went into the local florists ('Bette's Nosegays – Love In Bloom') to order regressive roses for Mummy on Mummy's Day, the place was packed with huge, tatooed, boiler-suited blokes buying gladdies for their Mums and I bet their Mums made King Kong look cosy. One old bird I met on a bus said she had these three six-foot sons and she clouted them regularly across the earholes and they hadn't forgotten her on Mother's Day in 20 years. Whereas your sweet, kind, democratic Mother Martha, who could not raise a hand in anger against her kiddiewinks, has never had a Mother's Day card in all her permissive life. Not that I want one, you understand.

Talking of mothers, mine writes to say she's coming to stay for a week, to buy her spring wardrobe. Evans Outsizes, Prepare to Meet Thy Doom. Mother on the shop floor has been known to make entire departments come out on strike. She believes that what shop assistants are for is to assist her, shopping. She also believes they are fascinated by any pearl of information that drops from her lips about herself, her family and her world views and she thinks they all love her. They love me at Harrods, she says, smiling like the Queen Mum. And she always, but always, returns every purchase exactly one week later. In fact, she's staying a week just to give herself time for returns. Spring shopping is my Mother's version of luring back the Sun God and everything she buys is an exact replica of everything she's already bought. Thank heavens I shan't be able to go with her this year, because of the baby. Last year I had to stand there lightly sweating as she hooted across the counter, 'I'll have two of them, dear, in Nigger Brown'.

Yours, blushing Knicker Pink,

Martha

15 April

Dear Mary

Well, I got it all wrong. Your bloke doesn't have a double-barrel surname, he has a double-barrel *first* name. Bobby-Joe from the Lone Star State and I'm mighty glad to make his acquaintance, yessiree. Though you can't blame me for not guessing, can you? There hasn't been a male in this United Kingdom with a double first name since Christopher Robin finished saying his prayers, booted his Nanny downstairs and changed his name to Alf. What in the world is a Texan doing, squatting in Sebastopol Terrace? And he plays the guitar a treat, you say. Now, Mary, you'd better watch yourself. You know you have this weakness for men who play musical instruments. An uncle of mine suffered the same way and had four disastrous marriages as a result. First he was seduced by Auntie Louise tinkling on the piano, then by Auntie Ruth sawing away on the violin, then Auntie Gwen booped at him with her clarinet and he ended up with a Ukrainian on the harmonica, who led him a dog's life until he went stone deaf and lived happily ever after.

It's all childhood conditioning, I think. I've spent hours singing the baby to sleep, getting myself well lodged in his inner ear. I rather fancy myself in the role, bending sweetly over the cradle, warbling away. Two bars of carry the lad who's born to be *King* over the sea to *Skye* and his dear little eyelids droop. Unfortunately for my ego, Ben can do the same thing with his record player. Eek, scrawk, crash, bang go the Clash and the baby's dear little eyelids droop. Lord knows, I actively long to be dispensable most of the time but when I am, it puts me out no end. I just adore that baby. He's so yummy at the moment I could eat him, munch his pink fingernails, nibble his teeny ears, crunch every one of his crisp little curls. Which reminds me, I was on the telephone once and I turned round, talking, and there was our hamster with one of her new-born half-way down her throat. It's a thin line we mothers tread between desirable physical manifestations of bodily affections and plain old-fashioned cannibalism.

Ben came in yesterday and said one of his Gerties (the white mice) looked a bit dead. The poor rodent was lying with all four paws in the air. That's not a bit dead, I said to Ben, that's one stiff mouse you've got there and it looks like it's been murdered. See that other Gertie with gore on its whiskers? Ben denied all, said dead Gertie and gory Gertie were best friends. Just then, his best friend Flanagan came pounding up the stairs, leapt on Ben's back, chopped him on the neck and clobbered him to the ground. *Quod erat demonstrandum*, I said, and left them to it. What *is* it with boys? For what purpose is God readying them, apart from being cut-throats, footpads, commodity brokers and other social menaces?

I've devoted my life to eliminating every undesirable masculine trait from Ben's Y-chromosomes and what's the result? He hasn't a sensitive bone in his body and is absolutely enraptured by violence. He and Flanagan spend hours telling each other exactly how they'd poke people's eyes out if they were going to poke people's eyes out and then lean back with sated grins, saying oh wow, that's *bad* man, that's really *bad*.

I must do better with the baby. Perhaps, this time round, I should be a working mother but what work can I get nearby? My friend Lorna, opposite, is retraining at the local hospital as an autopsy technician. Corpses are OK on flexi-hours but it's a dead-end job, she says. I think Lorna's getting callous. There is a woman two roads away who runs a warehouse called Annie's Attic full of junk and I mean junk. Singer sewing machines without the sewing machines, chairs without seats, lamps that lack all standards. Still, better than Habitat, and she might give me a job. She's a single parent, too – seems quite nice, what you can see of her under old cupboards.

Hey. Did you notice I said a single parent *too*? That's a giveaway and no wonder, with Josh disappearing at 8 am and reappearing at 9 pm or thereabouts. If I shuffled the baby in with four other babies, I doubt he could pick out his own with any confidence. Would he even notice if I gave it away? He might ask after it a few times – doing all right, is it, coming along nicely, is it? He'd probably only catch on a decade from now, because of the baby not being there to go to his Old School.

I am still shattered about Josh giving Tom the money to write *The Flasher's Guide to Feminism*. I didn't deign to ask how much but it rankles. I mean, what sort of vicious circle am I in? My ex being kept by my present spouse so that my ex can tell the world how ghastly it was to live with libby me and women like me. Josh says I must regard it as an investment and that he's merely trying to ensure me and the children of our rightful dues. He's actually drawn up some sort of contract about repayment of capital sum and royalties on the first so many thousand and rights on the paperback and heaven knows what else. What attitude should I take with Josh? Gratitude that he's protecting my interests, however misguidedly? Cynicism that he only wants to recoup what he's spent, supporting me and Tom's kids? Or silent contempt – I do a nice line in silent contempt.

Yours with worried blue eyes,

Martha

Cannibalism

Dear Mary

I thought we all agreed with Kate Millett that our Middle Eastern sisters needed our support in their battle to emerge from the veil and now you're saying Mo is back from Arabistan and you're both 'into chadors'. Mary, what can you and Mo *look* like, scuttling up and down Sebastopol Terrace covered from head to foot in black bags? What is appropriate in far-flung desert parts is hardly *comme il faut* up the Co-op. People will talk. People will come along in white jackets and take you away. And what on earth does poor Bobby-Joe make of it all? Just as he's getting to know you, you vanish behind folds of cloth, leaving him bereft of a single erogenous zone.

In some ways, of course, there is something rather appealing about the idea. Many's the time I've wanted to rush out of the house for a packet of fags and had to choose between getting all tarted up or going as I am and frightening the horses. Whereas if I could drop a black shroud all over myself, no one would know it was me. I'd just be a large black bundle padding through the streets, the ultimate asexual object. Instant privacy.

You know, the more I think about it, Mary, the more I think you and Mo may be on to something. Who's going to want to molest a shapeless mass? What man will whistle at an animated shroud? Talk about Reclaiming the Night – if we were wrapped up like that, they'd hand it back to us on a platter. We could get men to join in, too. That'd make rapists and muggers and other male disturbers of women's peace think twice. Imagine one of them pouncing on a black-draped siren from the mysterious East and finding, underneath, the heavyweight champion of Liverpool North? A couple of straight lefts and the beast would be put off sex and handbags for a good many moons.

And, apart from anything else, black figures flitting about in the night would put the fear of the Prophet into any man not about his rightful business. I've got an old black evening dress up in the attic and even I should be able to run up a chador. If it catches on, they might issue them on the National Health. Send me a snap of you in yours, so I can see what you don't look like.

I've had a great idea too, if a teeny bit macabre. You know my friend Lorna, the one who got a job as an autopsy technician and was rabbiting on about corpses fitting in so well with women's hours? I was pondering on this, thinking about a job for myself, when the bulb lit up. What is one of the very last bastions of male supremacy in the Western world, sans even a token woman? The Marines? The girls are in there. Miners? The girls are down there. Yes, you've got it. Undertaking. Have you ever seen or heard of a female undertaker? Ever caught a glimpse of a lady in a hearse, alive and well and looking mournful? And if not, why not? Women must have laid out corpses for hundreds of years and where are we now? Pushed back into the kitchen is where, cooking the funeral meats for the wake, muscled out of our rightful heritage by men.

So you know what I'm going to do? I'm going to find out what you have to do to be an undertaker (Apprenticeships? Day-release schemes? Evening classes?) and then I'm going to set up my own all-female business. Martha's Mortuary. Shiftwork only, ho ho. I think people would flock. I know I'd much rather put my body in the hands of women instead of some boring old fatty in a wing-collar and a top hat whom I wouldn't trust dead or alive. I'd be a sort of midwife, only the other way round; it's good steady work, ideally suited to family life and my clients could hardly object if I shut up shop now and then, in an emergency, could they? When you think about it, men being undertakers is positively unnatural. It's the same story as doctors, really. For generations, women attended at births and then, all of a sudden, a whole lot of men arrived, stethoscopes flapping, and gave us the heave-ho. Why shouldn't I be the first to reverse that takeover? I could combine it with wearing a chador, for that matter. What could look more decorously mournful than that?

I just told Josh my idea. That man has no imagination. First he said what would the Department think, him having a wife in Undertaking. Then he said if I was going to start a fashion in black sacks, it might seriously affect the sales of *The Flasher's Guide to Feminism* because what man would want to flash at a black sack? Josh, I said, that is the *whole* point. Pshaw, he said, or something like it, and disappeared into a black sulk.

I have to stop writing now. Ben has just decided it is time

The Grim Flasher

he showed me how independent he is by going camping this weekend alone, with Flanagan. So will I buy him a rucksack, get batteries for his torch, sew up the split in his groundsheet, wash his sleeping bag, find a camping site, look up the trains, pack oxtail soup, sausages, baked beans, drinking chocolate, long-life milk, Mars Bars, Coke, toilet paper, apples, soap, tin-opener, saucepans, fork, knife, spoon, plate, Brillo pads and drive him to the station. Please.

Two seconds later, Flanagan's Mum is on the phone. As I know, she says, she – Flanagan's Mum – is a working woman and hasn't the time to get Flanagan equipped for the weekend. So will I, very kindly, get him oxtail soup, sausages, baked beans, torch batteries, drinking chocolate te tum te tum te tum. The nerve of these working women. What does she think I do all day long? Sit around in a face pack? Martha's Mortuary, here I come.

Yours, banging on death's door,

Martha

Dear Mary

Thanks for the snap you sent me in your last letter of you and Mo in chadors outside Sebastopol Terrace. You're quite right, I can't tell which is you and which is Mo, but why is my bewilderment merely 'a predictable bourgeois individualist reaction'? Even a duck-billed platypus might become a trifle disorientated if it couldn't pick out its pal in the next burrow from any duck-billed platypus that happened to wander by. I know, I wrote that chadors could have their advantages but this is ridiculous.

Do you suppose Iranian soldiers fighting in Iraq carry photos of their womenfolk back home that they can't tell from their enemy's women, never mind their friends? If so, it must be pretty boring for them back at the barracks. Here, have a look at my Fatimah, mate, says one, passing over a pic of black washing. Cor, smashing, says the mate, have a shufti at my old lady then, and down the line goes another Polaroid pin-up of laundry in vaguely human form. Anonymity in the streets is one thing but this kind of dressing could mean a man gets his meals cooked for a fortnight before he realizes his wife's moved out and his mother-in-law's moved in.

I dare say that proves a vital point about the interchangeability of women's servicing roles but it's not one I can contemplate without feeling a bad identity crisis coming on. Besides, I showed your photo to Josh and you wouldn't have liked his reaction one bit. He thought it was quite sexy. All cats are grey in the chador, he said wittily. They're obviously his version of throwing the car keys in the pool and gambling on who'd be in his bed that night. How do you know Bobby-Joe isn't fantasizing that he's got Mo under the blankets? Well, not Mo, perhaps. Raquel Welch?

I'm sorry I didn't write back immediately, but the life of a housewife is not conducive to outside interaction. What is it conducive to, I often ask myself? Sometimes I think I might as well reside permanently in a pot-hole for all the contact I have with the great panorama of twentieth-century events, including women's liberation. The microscopic happenings in

Home Sweet Home so distort all perspective that I frequently feel I'd happily swop the Sex Discrimination Act for any suggestion of what to cook for dinner that doesn't include spaghetti and meat balls.

Being a 100 per cent wife and mother feels a bit like living on Mars and trying to take an intellectual interest in world affairs on a planet 80 light years away. An interesting mental exercise, perhaps, like playing Scrabble in Latin, but equally irrelevant. You and Mo can easily live on a diet of abstract theory because nothing in your actual life looms up to confound you. But if I put the smallest liberating idea into action the backlash knocks me sideways before I can get the words out. Like I told Josh I was going to bed early and he'd have to give the baby his last feed. Which he did but forgot to change nappies so the poor little thing has nappy rash again.

I know I could push on until Josh got it right but the baby doesn't have Third Party Indemnity and how many personal battles can I fight over an increasingly raw but innocent bum? Again, I perfectly realize that I was not put on this earth in order to keep the fruit of my loins unendingly supplied with toilet paper but I fear I am already as conditioned as Pavlov's canines. One cry of despair from the smallest room and I'm rushing about shouting *mea culpa* and shredding up newspapers for the incarcerated loved one. Well, not shouting *mea culpa*, perhaps, but feeling it.

I'll admit it does them no good but how to break out of the vicious circle? I send Ben out to buy two pounds of leeks and he comes back, five minutes later, saying, 'What do leeks look like?' Ben, I say, how can you exist in the twentieth century and not know what leeks look like? Being conversant, if indeed you are, with Newton's Theory of Gravity, the Pythagoras Theorem, and the cycle of DNA, will simply not suffice. Leeks have their place in the History of Human Achievement, even if you can't get A-levels in them. It may be a humble place, unsung, unrewarded, not in the running for a Nobel Prize, but place it is.

A male who can pick out a goodly leek and process it into a Lancashire Hot Pot may possibly contribute more to the struggle for sexual equality than any amount of ideological jargon. You tell me, Mary, that your Bobby-Joe is a truly feminist man because he always says he *and* she, his *and* hers, men *and* women. Hurrah for Bobby-Joe. But can he pick out a decent leek at ten paces and make of it something fit to be ladled into mankind's (humankind's) mouth? If so, full marks. If not, hot air. And answer me this one. Who cleans

the lavatory at Sebastopol Terrace – No, don't fudge it with ifs and buts. Who, Mary?

In case you think I'm putting you down, I shall nobly admit that my money is not yet where my mouth is, not by a long chalk. You remember my telling you about the ludicrous Studs, that B-movie twit my friends were all swooning about? The one that calls them 'chick' and tweaks their bottoms? He came round unexpectedly the other evening when Josh was working late. Well, Josh is always working late. Anyway, he sat at my kitchen table, swilled my beer, called me 'beauty' and said nothing turned him on like a woman in the full bloom of maturity with her hands dug into a bowl of flour.

Actually, I had just decanted a Betty Crocker Cake Mix (add one egg and stir) but did I let on? I did not. You'd have thought I was making a week's wholemeal granary loaves, the way I got kneading. The man's a fool, of course, wearing that silly hat pulled down over one eye, talking in a fake American accent, either drunk or pretending to be. But I have the feeling, Mary, that under all that tough-guy stuff, Studs is just shy. Just a big, shy boy. He put his arm round my waist at one point and I gave a girlish giggle. I suppose I should have smacked him. Please send one chador knitting pattern, by return of post.

Yours, with needles poised,

Martha

Dear Mary

I've had this man Kev in all week repainting the stairwell because Josh said it looked like a stretch of the H-Block, what with the scuffs and gouges made by Ben and his elfin friends flitting upstairs. Between brush strokes, Kev has been giving me the benefit of his thoughts on the rich tapestry of life and my blood, Mary, is only just uncongealing.

The way I see it, Marf, says Kev, any man could kill one woman in an off moment, know what I mean? No, Kev, I say. Like if she's getting on his wick like. Nagging and that, says Kev. But this Ripper, topping 13 women, that's a bit much, know what I mean, Marf? No, Kev, I say. Well, there's a lot of Rippers about, Marf. Take this man goes to my pub. He's got a very funny attitude to women. I reckon he could be a Ripper soon as look at you. At me you mean, Kev, I say. Right, Marf, says Kev.

Well, this man, he bought this python. Ten pound a foot, he paid, so he's got about sixty quids' worth of python there and he brings it in the pub and he sits there with it, drinking his usual Pernod, Guinness and bitter. First thing, it wraps itself round this dog and the dog's yipping away and this woman starts shouting. Shut your mouth, you old cow, he says, and the publican says don't you talk like that to my mother, and there's a bit of a barney, but it settles down because nobody wants to call the police, due to this and that, you know. Anyway, then all the gels start coming in and shrieking when they see the python and throwing up their hands and spilling their drinks and this man is smiling away. He likes that, see? Giving all the gels a good scare.

But then, Marf, these other two gels come in and they're different. Oh, they say, look at that snake, Rosie. Oh, isn't it beautiful. And off they go, billing and cooing away at the thing and this bloke starts frowning. Then, all of a sudden, he bends down, picks up the python by its neck, drags it over to the bar, and thumps its head against the side until it's dead. It was like the python was only good for scaring the gels and when a couple of them weren't scared, that was the end of the python. Funny, eh? Takes all sorts, doesn't it, Marf? Yes, Kev, I say.

And that's not all, Mary. Kev says he reckons there are more nutters in front of bars than behind them and I reckon he's right and I reckon Kev's one of them. Two days later, he starts coming down from his ladder and telling me he can see Prince Philip's face on the ceiling. Next thing, he sees the whole Royal Family, up to and including Lady Di. Not surprisingly, the experience seemed to unhinge him. He didn't turn up this morning, so I've now got a stairwell blocked with ladders and pots and old sheets and Mother's arriving some time today, which is one of the reasons we started repainting in the first place.

I dread it. She'll be on the warpath within seconds, wanting to know what I've done to Josh to drive him away evenings, picking up the baby and saying 'poor little thing' as if it were Third World and asking Jane what's wrong with her legs that she can't wear skirts. Already she's pushed me several notches below depression level by suggesting, on the phone, that I have a face lift. Mother, I said (shocked out of saying Mummy for a change), I don't need a face lift. I'm 38, you know, not 101. That's as may be, she said, but if you leave it, the price will go up. Mother, I said, I can't lift a face that's got no lift yet, just because it'll cost me twice the money in 10 years, can I? It's Josh I'm thinking of, she said enigmatically and put the phone down. Two whole tears dripped down my nose. A week of her and it'll take a 10-ton crane to lift my face. Then Jane comes in and moans about Granny visiting. Don't talk like that about your grandmother, Jane, I hear myself say, I won't have it. Mary, sometimes I can feel my personality splitting.

Of course, I've done quite the wrong thing, mother-wise, getting the house looking reasonably nice. Your mother, Mary, is never going to come and stay at Sebastopol Terrace, is she? I can't see her coping with bare floorboards and that rat you say keeps popping up round the dustbins, no matter how cute you think he is. Has it occurred to you that what you think is one rat is actually twenty rats all looking alike? If I were you, I'd send for the rodent exterminator now, before one of them nips a hole in your waterbed and drowns you in your sleep.

Yesterday, I started on a round of phone calls to try to get Ben a place in some college if he does decide to leave school this summer with anything more academic than one CSE grade five. The first place I called, they put me through to the Department of Vocational Something-or-other and someone picked up the phono, said, 'I wouldn't do that course, if I were you, it's worse than useless,' and banged it down. Great confidence, that's inspired. Who was it? A disaffected student? An Illich de-schooler? A Tory mole? You've never had to plough through these college brochures, Mary, and you can thank your lucky stars. You need a degree, these days, just to work out how to get one. A degree, I mean. Oh God, there goes the doorbell. Hang on.

That was Mother, complete with twenty-four shopping bags, no change for the taxi and a foot already firmly stuck in one of Kev's paint pots.

Yours, wishing I had house room for a python,

Martha

Poor
little
thing

20 May

Dear Mary

I'm alone at last, in the stilly night. The babe has crashed out after the hard graft of jigging his cot 68 times across the room, Mother after the hard graft of seeing Harrods, and Josh after the hard graft of seeing Mother. I have just committed the mortal sin of switching on the central heating again so that I can take off two cardies and write to you. Josh did his usual Switching-off Ceremony at the end of March, leaving me and the baby the only two Eskimos in the old home igloo – the rest of them bundle off mornings to their various snuggeries and arrive home after work fanning themselves and saying phew, bit stuffy in here isn't it?

Josh's Department, Thatcherites to a man, has responded to the Leader's call for cuts by awarding him a secretary all his very own – until now he's had to make do with the dryads of the typing pool. Not that he mentioned this little perk to me. I called him last Thursday to say should I pay the electricity bill, since it was now an apoplectic purple and, instead of him, got this deep frozen Benenden voice that managed to fight congenital lock jaw long enough to inform me that himself was tied up at the moment. On the verge of saying we must all snatch our pleasures where we can, I lost my nerve and couldn't even bring myself to say I was his wife. Simply couldn't face playing that golden oldie role, the Trouble and Strife, interrupting His Godliness with some boring domestic plaint like it was his turn to peel the potatoes tonight. So I said ay am Lord Dewberry's sekerety, ay hev His Lordship on the laine, and was put through pronto.

Josh was noticeably unamused but too canny to give the game away. When I asked could he pick up ravioli round the Italian on his way home, he said three bags full Lord Dewberry, dinner tonight it *is*, and rang off. What's more, he didn't have a chance to harangue me when he did get home because, just as he was opening his mouth, in sailed Mother to engulf him in her bosom, murmuring *dear* Joshua in that hushed voice she always uses on him, as if he were suffering terminal martyrdom. Marthadom?

She really has it in for me at the moment, that auld Mother o'Mine – something about the spring and the flowering sukebind always turns her against me. Yesterday, staggering back from a full day's shopperama wearing a new hat in the likeness of a squashed mushroom, she demanded, out of the blue, to be told how many pairs of socks Joshua had. Mother, I said, search me. Upon which she delivered herself of a moving speech about the fearful fragility of marriages when wives did not even know how many pairs of socks their husbands had. Loyally, I forebore to say that her precious Josh was one of those persons who wore his shirts tucked into his underpants, which fact, in any properly run country with a reasonable representation of females at the pinnacles of power, would constitute grounds for instant divorce. That and wearing shirt collars folded back over jackets and socks with sandals – matrimonial killers, every one.

Some minutes later, she took a shufti up our stairwell and said she didn't know how dear Joshua could possibly work with paint pots and ladders all over the landing. Josh, I said, goes to an office to work, Mother. A warm, tastefully furnished, close-carpeted bijou technological miracle called an office. It's me, Mother, that works in a hell of paint pots and ladders. Me.

Undeterred, she went on to say that she had tried telephoning me to tell me what time her train arrived but I had been out. Pause for implications to sink in. Daughter is Scarlet Woman, spends daylight hours togged out in Y-front frocks chatting up lounge lizards in sleazy Mayfair drinking clubs when should be suckling innocent babe and meeting clean-living Away-Day Mother at Liverpool Street. However. She had then phoned dear Joshua and got this charming girl who'd said Josh couldn't meet her due to dining with Lord Dewberry that night. Wasn't it nice, said Mother, that Joshua had such contacts and nicer still that he'd foresworn them in order to welcome his Mother-in-Law and she only hoped I appreciated him as much as she did.

You're always saying, Mary, that feminists should make friends with their mothers, but where do I begin? What possible way can I introduce mine to the Women's Movement? Say to her, Mother, do you realize you are a member of an oppressed class? Mother, who's squashed Father so flat all his life that he looks like a piece of lasagna with a moustache on one end? Mother, who wouldn't recognize oppression if it leapt up and garotted her? I read

Nancy Friday's book *My Mother, My Self*, and all I could think was how lucky she was, having such an amenable mother.

Anyway, the baby likes Mother. He's done nothing ever since she arrived but gurgle at her like something out of the Wonderful World of Disney. Good as gold, says Mother, I don't know *what* you complain about, oo's a luvvy babby den, coochy, coochy coo. Personally, I wouldn't be surprised if, somehow, the baby's dummy ends up half-way down her throat quite soon.

Yours matricidally,

Martha

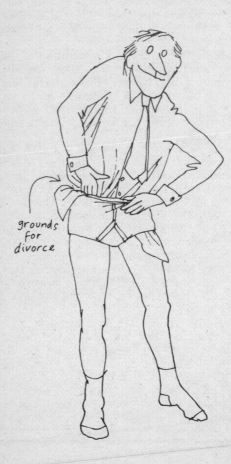

grounds
for
divorce

Dear Mary

I have to hand your anthropological dissertation on The Role of Shopping in the Establishment of Female Bonding Mechanisms, for which no thanks. Men, you assure me, hunt, drink, tell dirty jokes, and observe footballs being moved about in order to coment masculine bonds. Ergo, I must be prepared to hump myself through Horrid's Jewellery Dept to achieve the same end with women, viz my Mother. Great. Help yourself to a PhD in putting down Marthas.

You've overlooked one tiny detail, though. Said men, in the pursuance of said bonding, take it for granted that the necessary rites are carried out together. Like they *all* shoot rabbits and Germans, they *all* swig beer, tell the one about the landlady's daughter, and yell themselves silly at Wembley. Whereas I am unable fully to participate in the Shopping Rite because (a) I haven't got the money and (b) I haven't got the money. A fact that makes one more unbridgeable gap between Mother and me.

My lack of the readies merely proves to her that I have led my disgustingly promiscuous (twice-married) life in vain since the only justification, in her view, for promiscuity or marriage or men in general is that the women who go in for them come out clutching enough lolly to buy up Horrid's Jewellery Dept. In the name of the Father, the Son, and the HG, of course. As Mother is fond of pointing out, she is a Christian woman.

Anyway, how come you're suddenly in favour of conspicuous female consumption? Whatever happened to Betty Freidan and her Feminine Mystique? Betty F's whole point was that all the Mr Bigs of industry and advertising were in a conspiracy to keep women in the home so that they could be sold things and now you're saying I should let them have their way with me. True, there is only one thing more boring than being a woman at home being sold things and that is being a woman at home *not* being sold things but it's the principle that counts. Isn't it?

The fact is, Mary, that you haven't got your finger on the

nation's economic pulse and no wonder. You squat rent-free in Sebastopol Terrace. Your electricity reaches you gratis, due to some nifty intervention by Bobby-Joe between the mains and your bulbs. Your food is lifted by nimble-fingered Mo (I know *property* is theft but where does a leg of lamb fit in, wafted out of the Co-op under Mo's chador?) and you fulfil the rest of your needs (ciggies, dope, sound) courtesy the dole. Which is not what I call grasping the harsh realities of Thatcher's Britain. I, on the other hand, live cheek by jowl with them, sustained only by hand-outs from Josh, courtesy the Department. And believe me, once you've joined the system, press-ganged by marriage and parenthood, the Good Ship Lolly soon Pops.

Take mortgages, for example. Our annual statement dropped on the mat this week to the cackles of the robber barons who lurk, these days, under the thoroughly respectable label 'Building Society'. Huge monthly sums go out in payment, the figures in the Balance column dwindle nicely and just as the mortgaged heart begins to soar – whoomp – it gets shot down by 'Interest' at the bottom, which pushes the Balance up again to almost exactly where it was before you started – out of sight. In the last twelve months we've paid out over three thousand pounds and managed to increase our actual ownership of this pile of bricks by exactly £394.98. At this rate, I'll be a heap of whitened bones before we own half the front door. Josh, it would appear, is working for nothing and if *he* is working for nothing, matie, what about me? What's ten times nothing? I've got a device for re-using bits of old soap now. You stick them all in a plastic thingie, dunk the thingie in hot water and press down, whereupon one brand-new piece of soap is supposed to emerge. In fact, you get a ghastly gollop of goo that looks like something the cat brought up – you see the lengths I'm forced to go?

The only ray of light this week was Studs calling round again, which should tell you something about the general state of gloom. In he rolls, fingers extended like a mad crayfish, ready for tweaking. Hello, Gorgeous, he hoots. How's my honey chile, honey baby, honey honey? Shriek, I go. Bridle, giggle. Things look distinctly up. Then I fetch him a beer from the kitchen and when I get back, he's started on Jane. Not that Jane is in any danger. Cut it out, *creep*, she's shouting in her usual forthright way. How I admire my daughter. How my heart sank. But the bitter end came when Mother appeared in her squashed mushroom hat. You're

Martha's *Mother*? says Studs, pretending to fall off his chair. Come *on*, baby, pull the other one. Sister, I'll believe, but *Mother* – who are you kidding? And Mother titters. She pats her hair and titters, while I stand there feeling like the pensioned-off wife in the harem.

Still, I'll say one thing for Studs. He doesn't give a toss if a woman looks like a piece of pumice stone, outweighs an elephant and is all of ninety-four. As long as she's a living, breathing female, he's in business. Is that the worst sort of sexism or should he be awarded some kind of medal for the world's most undiscriminatory behaviour?

Yours, only asking,

Martha

CREEP!

Dear Mary

Mother departed yesterday and in the resulting burst of euphoria I snuggled up to Josh and said would he love me just as much if I were cross-eyed, knock-kneed and had sticky-out ears and he said no. And I said you promised to love me till death did us part and now you're saying cross-eyes knock-knees and sticky-out ears would us part and he said he wasn't saying any such thing and I said he was and he said he wasn't and why was I being so illogical and I said I wasn't illogical and he said *women* and I said *men*. Then the neighbour's little girl came in to return some sugar and said what was the cat's name and I said Bimby and she said no, but what is its *real* name and I said to Josh isn't that marvellous, she knows the cat isn't *really* called Bimby and he said he called it Bimby and I said she means who is the cat *really*, to other cats, and he said oh God! and went upstairs. I think I'll have to join the Bhagwan and go orange, there's no understanding around here of the mysteries of life.

Then I had words with the children about fruit. I do not know the solution to fruit. I come home with two pounds of apples, a pound of satsumas and a bunch of bananas. I arrange them beautifully on a white platter in the middle of the table. Then Ben and Jane come in and reach for them and I say no, leave them, I've just bought them and they say I'm always saying leave them and then, when everything's gone all shrivelled, I say *eat* them for goodness sake, so what do I want? What none of them realizes is that fruit and food and things in the fridge and tins in the cupboard don't get there by magic. There isn't a good fairy about, waving her wand and, hey presto, baked beans and bunches of bananas. There's just me, Martha, making lists, slogging down to the shops and slogging back again. All they know is, they go out, come back and the cupboard's full. Magic.

Probably that's why I came home today from the supermarket with a hot toothbrush. I don't believe in your 'property is theft' stuff, I just have this very deep feeling that the world owes me something, even if it's only one yellow toothbrush, medium bristle. The thing is, buying provisions for five people week after week after week is an indeterminate sentence to hard labour. First, I have to check everything that's running out. Then the baby has to be parked with my neighbour because, otherwise, he'd get so squashed under tins they'd have to sell him off as battered goods, half-price. So all the time I'm shopping, I've got this little picture in my mind of him, mouth open, chest heaving, face purple, neighbour's hands closing round his throat, like a silent horror movie. Then I have to drag my bag-on-wheels down to the supermarket, get lumbered with the trolley with the stuck wheels that keeps forcing me round in a circle, fight through the aisles, load up with stuff I wouldn't be seen dead eating (Sugar Puffs, prune purée, sickly orange drinks), hang about in an endless queue, unload everything at the check-out, load everything again on the other side, pay out ridiculous sums for the privilege and then collapse with a silent but painful stroke.

So what I feel is the supermarket ought to reward me for working so hard on their behalf and, since they don't, I am forced to reward myself. Hence the toothbrush. They pretend they're doing us a favour, having everything self-service, and all the time it's us doing them a favour, trekking round their noisy, overcrowded food hangars so we can stick our week's housekeeping in their tills and pay for their plastic bags covered with their advertising. There was this old lady in there today, doing it her way. Not sticking toothbrushes up her jumper but quietly awarding herself consoling swigs of whisky while struggling to buy Whiskas for her moggy. By the time she arrived at the check-out, that old lady was feeling no pain and the bottle was tucked neatly back on the drinks shelf, a little bit empty. I gave her an admiring grin as I passed her. Bottoms up, she said, bless her OAP heart. What supermarkets ought to do, if they had any imagination beyond fleecing you, is give each worn-out trolley-pusher a prezzie at check-out. A pair of tights, a bag of sweeties, a toothbrush, free. It'd cost them less than shoplifting and cut down on that, too.

Glad to hear you've graduated from your Sub-Orgasmic Therapy Group. I'd have sent you a card, except they don't make cards to mark such earth-moving occasions, even in these permissive days. Something tasteful and discreet, like roses are red, violets are blue, Spring has come and so have you. Personally – and I'm not underestimating your triumph – I find the Big O soon sinks to the level of yet another household chore. Part of a list that goes 'buy green thread, spray apple tree, iron shirts, have orgasm'. Sort of a duty, really, that you owe your beloved, like buying polyunsaturated marge for his cholesterol level and sticking Vic up his nose for a cold. Still, at least your union with Bobby-Joe is not yet sacred, like mine with Josh, so you've got a little room for manoeuvre left, if you see what I mean.

Nevertheless, rising from the sub-orgasmic depths into the bright white light of fulfilled womanhood doesn't necessarily give you the go-ahead to include my private habits in your Exploring Politics Through the Sexual Act project. But more of that in my next.

Yours, in wifely modesty,

Martha

Dear Mary

I've been brooding about those fairy tales where Snow White, Sleeping Beauty, the Ice Queen, the Little Mermaid and other happily resting ladies get woken from their snoozes by a peck from Prince Right on the old liperoos. Male fantasies about arousing female virgins, what? But did anyone inform the ladies in question that once they're presented with the result of their awakened passions – ie a permanently insomniac infant – all they will desire in life is to return from whence they came?

The Princes I've kissed, hoping they'll turn into frogs on account of frogs don't disturb your kip like Princes do. In fact, my idea of a happy ending is a Prince whose kiss works the other way round and puts me to sleep for a hundred years, by Royal Decree. And if any wicked fairy is presently hanging about, aching to stick me with a spindle and several thousand years of shut-eye, she's only got to say and my Welcome mat is out.

OK, so I'm fatigued, whacked, bushed, zonked and clapped-out. As my friend Dorrie Carrie Bogvak often says since becoming a Mother in the US of A, Sleep? I'd kill for it. She had twins, poor dear, which guarantees her an unravell'd sleeve of care for life. My darling issue has taken to waking just as my eyelids close, with many a glad cry of whoop de do, bring on the girls, who's for tennis and such. I, needless to say, am his one wan guest, sole subject for his experiments in sleep deprivation.

Josh, woken just one time by my ninety-eighth nocturnal excursion, reared up long enough to ask how he was expected to support us all if he was *continually* disturbed and fell back unconscious again, leaving me petrified. Was this masculine blackmail or was it true? Admittedly, he's cross with me at the moment because he came back from the dentist with a frozen face and I didn't notice the difference but what *would* we do if he was laid off for incipient drowsiness? There's a lot of laying off about, these days.

Only yesterday he complained about his boss, Irene, the

one who looks like a Thirties film star. Not a great Thirties film star, you understand, just a B-grade Accompanying Feature. Anyway, Ms Bossy-boots has presented him with this form to fill in, assessing his own worth to the Department. It's got questions like 'List, in order of importance, the personal characteristics you possess that offer most value to your Unit' and 'What, in your opinion, is the optimum staffing level for your Unit?' I mean, why doesn't she just hand him a pearl-inlay pistol and tell him she's sure he'll do the honourable thing, like they did in the good old days? Then he could shoot her in the back and plead womanslaughter on the grounds of diminished responsibility (his) and ameliorated nagging (hers), excuses all judges find perfectly acceptable when men murder women.

The thing is, Mary, I thought she fancied him. I said as much to Josh and he muttered on a bit about how Irene is jealous of his new secretary, Cassandra by name and, I dare say, by nature. What evidence has Irene got for that idea, I asked in my professionally objective voice (a banshee shriek) and, with that, we were into a goodly bit of overtime bickering until Josh flaked out and the baby, bright-eyed and bushy-tailed, flaked in. From then on, in between poker games, chorus girls, the popping of champagne corks and all the other debaucheries of nursery night-life, I kept eyeing Josh's prone and snoring form. Could this protuberance under the blankets that I call Husband possibly arouse, in female office bosoms, the pitter-patter of passion?

Speaking of which, you asked me about my sex life, re your Exploring Politics Through the Sexual Act project. Fascinated to hear how you and Bobby-Joe practise Marxist dialectics in bed – him being Thesis, you being Antithesis and, whoopee, here comes Synthesis. Also you being the Shadow Cabinet and him being Benn and you being the EEC and Bobby-Joe implementing Conference decisions. What do Social Democrats do? Say American Express, that'll do nicely? Anyway, just put Josh and me down as having no politics to speak of at the moment, unless you count border skirmishes with him being Israel and me being the Lebanon. Personally, I reckon I'm No-Man's-Land till the baby's grown and then I'll be in a wheelchair, though I dare say there are things you can do in wheelchairs we wot not of.

To add to my burdens, Jane has taken to her bed with what she calls the glandulars and I call skiving off. She lies there in the bombsite of her bedroom looking like the wreck of the *Hesperus* and stuffing herself with Curiously Strong

The Fisherman's Friend.

Mints, the Fisherman's Friend. Some devoted and clearly certifiable young man appeared at the door on the second day of her withdrawal from the world, holding a bunch of flowers. As he entered her room, I heard Jane say 'Oh God, it's you. Oh do piff off.' The poor wretch starts backing out, his crest all fallen and, blow me down if she doesn't then shout after him 'Leave the flowers, you nerd.'

And he does. Slinks back again, dumps the bouquet and scuttles out, saying sorry to the wallpaper all the way down the stairs. Jane, I said after he'd gone, equality is one thing but this is ridiculous. A man takes the trouble to visit you in your bed of pain and you tell him to piff off and leave the flowers. More fool him, she says, swallowing ten more Fisherman's Friends. What, I wonder, would Barbara, Queen of Cartland, make of Jane?

Yours, not wishing to hear the answer,

Martha

Dear Mary

If we lived in the Middle Ages, I'd have the Black Death. As we don't, my red eyes, grey gums and black tongue must be due to the bout of sorrow-drowning I had last night. Not that any got drowned. On the contrary, several new ones rose to the surface like three-day corpses. The occasion was a dinner party given at the house of one Nigel, colleague of Josh, to exhibit his collection of Top People and put up with the odd Bottom Person like me, admitted on inspection of my marriage lines.

My sorrows started back at mill, as I'm putting on my sexy black number. Josh stops in front of me, eyes my cleavage and says that shows too much bust. *Bust.* My blood ran cold. Josh, I said, ladies in corset departments have busts. Mother has a bust. But when I, Martha, mate of your choice and sharer of your duvet, have a bust, all is over between us. Taking no notice, Josh adds that he thinks it's time the baby was weaned. You ought to stop, Martha, he says. Stop what? I said. Bustfeeding? Martha, *please*, he says, let's try not to be late again.

So I conceal the offending bust and the broken heart under a fringed paisley shawl and silently we drive off, to be met at a wee £200,000 Hampstead cottage by Caroline, mine hostess. Caroline leans foward when she talks and opens her eyes very wide, as if to convince you she's terribly awake. Nigel leans back and closes his eyes very tight, as if to convince you he's not. So nice, says Caroline, bug-eyed. Lovely, says Nigel, lids vacuuming in. Upon which, the fringe of my shawl snakes out, hooks itself to the front door latch and resists two minutes' tugging before it gives in. Ricocheting free, I burst in upon the party but not before the fringe has grabbed an umbrella from a stand and draped it tastefully at my left hip.

Next, I am clasped to the chest of a passing military man as the fringe entwines itself in his jacket button. He is forced to divest himself, I say we've got to stop meeting like this, Josh frowns. Undeterred, the fringe leaps at the watch strap of a young man dispensing drinks. I say I didn't know you cared, Josh frowns a lot more. Then I bend maternally over a small pyjama'd girl (Martha's so good with children), the fringe molests her, she breaks into sobs and several adults have to tear her away. I say how's that for a little fringe theatre, Josh pulls off my shawl with quite unnecessary violence and my bust is released for the evening.

From these squalid scenes, we progress to the dining table and I am seated next to a gent in a blazer and an extremely hostile moustache. During the next thirty minutes, through gazpacho, poached salmon, petit pois and duchesse potatoes, he tells me about sparking plugs. By the time the strawberries arrive, I know more about sparking plugs than whoever invented sparking plugs and, at the advent of the cheese board, the worm turns. I start telling him about the baby. I tell him all I know about the baby, what the baby eats and what the baby refuses to eat. I hold forth at length upon the baby's little ways. I am very animated about the baby, he is strangely still. As the brandy is poured, he heaves himself round to the woman on his left and leaves me alone, at last, with my Remy Martin.

And, believe it or not, Josh has noticed and Josh minds. What came over me, he asks when we get home. Do I not realize that men at parties are not interested in hearing about babies? Have I not learned that babies are hardly the ideal coin of conversational currency? That I have, Josh, I say. I am deeply cognizant of that fact. When a man's eyeballs glaze, when he stares at the edge of my right earlobe, when he fidgets like a soul with itching powder up his Y-fronts, Martha gets the message. Man is bored, says the message. And what do I care, says Martha. Does man recognize when woman is bored? He does not. He refuses even to contemplate that sparking plugs are not everyone's favourite thing. Fair do's I said to that man, do you have children? Yes, he said. Well, I don't have sparking plugs so Heads I win.

Why, oh husband, is it shameful of me to bore a man rigid at a party by talking babies and not shameful at all for him to bore me rigid talking of sparking plugs? Martha, said Josh, you've had too much to drink. Possibly, Josh, I said. That is, I grant you, a remote possibility and then I fell down.

I expect no sympathy from you, Mary, in recounting this sombre tale. I dare say, given such a splendid choice, you might plump for sparking plugs over babies. Nevertheless, there's a moral in there somewhere, if only my head would stop hitting me long enough to let me see it.

It's a mad mad world. One day, my newspaper informs me that a handwriting expert, in possession of a scrap of Lady Diana's correspondence, has proclaimed the astonishing fact that her loops and stems show Lady Di is 'not career-minded'. She has no career in mind, you hear me, Mary? Being Queen of England, with your head all over stamps and five-pound notes (albeit several feet below your Master) is not a career. At heart, Lady Di is a homebody who wishes no more than to stay at home for the rest of her life cooking toad-in-the-hole for hubby and ironing his socks.

That settled, I read this review of a biography of Edgar Allen Poe. Poe, said the reviewer, 'was cursed with a streak of self-destruction which prevented him ever succeeding at anything'. Aahh, I said to Josh. Shame, isn't it? I can't hardly bear it, thinking about E. A. Poe and how unsuccessful he was. Makes me realize just how fortunate I am, being this uncareer-minded housewife, peas in a pod with the highest Lady in the Land and being so much more successful than E. A. Poe. My goodness me, Mary, some people have all the luck.

Yours, counting her blessings,

Martha

forward thrust

anti-matter

Nigel and Caroline drifting in Space.

Dear Mary

Just because Mr Begin dropped a few bombs on Iraq's nuclear piles doesn't mean he's about to dedicate his life to CND, you know. The idea of you and Mo shedding your chadors, discovering your Jewish grannies, and vowing to shop-lift only Israeli avocados from now on makes me think the two of you have finally gone critical yourselves.

Menachim is only breaking the other boys' toys before they can break his, anyway, and he's not going to be interested in your plan for an Israeli task force that zooms about the planet demolishing nuclear bases. Though, mind you, it'd be nice if *someone* would. I get quite frantic, sometimes, dosing the baby with vitamins and orange juice and knowing, all the while, that his future is really dependent on some male killer-ape ensconced in a barbed-wire desert with his hairy great finger an inch away from The Button.

I told Josh I wanted to take the baby and go on a CND march this summer and he said no I couldn't, it wasn't Department policy. What *is* Department policy then? I said. Letting babies frizzle in their cots like Kentucky Fried Chickens? Having women and children running through the streets like so many living torches?

Do you realize, I said, that the only people likely to survive a nuclear holocaust are those that started it in the first place? Out they'll all burrow from their underground sewers, twitching their horrid little tatty whiskers while the last rays of the nuclear sun twinkle on their military brass and medals and you know what they'll do? If any unfortunate corpse shows signs of life, they'll bend over it, shout 'Stand to attention you nasty little person' and the whole awful process will start all over again.

Honestly, that's about the only consolation I can think of for not surviving. Getting an invitation card saying the Ronald Reagans, the Leonid Brezhnevs, a few dozen boring old Generals and their ghastly yes-men request the pleasure of your company on a burnt-out planet. RSVP. Enough to make anyone pray for a quick end.

Besides, I said, I'll bet the Department has got its shelter planned. I'll bet its shelves are stocked with Heinz Baked Beans, Kellogg's Cornflakes, and ten billion Sainsbury's pink toilet rolls. What, Josh? Hey, Josh. *Speak* to me, Josh.

But you know what, Mary? Answer came there none. What Josh actually replied was did I know we'd run out of bread? Oh dearie me, I said. Now that is a tragedy. Why, the tears are prickling behind my eyeballs just to hear you say that. How can I possibly contemplate anything more hideous than us running out of bread, unless it's you and Irene and your lady secretary cuddling together in the Department's nuclear shelter while your family fry outside.

I expect you'll feel it incumbent upon you to take Irene as a mate, afterwards, on the grounds that it's your citizen's duty to repopulate the earth with the clones of the kind of citizens that booked seats in nuclear shelters to begin with. Going on a CND March, I said, may not be that much of a jolly for the baby, jogging up and down on my back for a hundred miles, but what's the point staying home, measuring his feet to make sure his shoes fit, when, one day soon, he won't have any feet to fit shoes to?

I went over the top a bit, there, I'll admit. To make matters worse, two minutes later there was Irene, knocking her knuckles on the front door. Irene — Josh's boss and token woman by appointment to HM. In she comes, sits herself down, has a little man-talk with her employee about things too esoteric for my ears, and then puts all her papers ostent-atiously away, smiling brilliantly at me the while as if to say the Big People have finished, now, let Children's Hour commence.

I flop down, green with exhaustion after cleaning up the baby, swabbing down the house, and cook, cook, cooking a three-course meal. Upon which, Josh swings his arm slowly out towards a bottle of wine, asks me if I'd like a glass, I say ta, and you know what Ms Bossieboots contributes at that moment in time? Aren't you lucky, Martha, she says, having a husband who spoils you so?

I sit staring at her, jaw at half-mast, while the real me picks up a machine gun, shouts Banzai and riddles her with bullets. Josh gives a cute and deprecating wiggle of his shoulders, meaning you *see*, Martha? Some people appre-ciate me. And the witch stays on for dinner because she says oh my how she miss   family life. I imagine her family drove her out with rakes and hoes and pickaxe handles some time ago.

That night my innards tore free of their moorings and cantered about like wild things. Josh, on the other hand, being of a forgiving nature, felt like a bit of how's your father. Have you ever tried to make love with a mouthful of Rennies, Mary? Don't.

There's Josh being the Sheik of Araby and there's me going chomp chomp and trying to give him a CSE Grade I kiss without losing my lozenges. Finally, Josh stops what he's doing and says Martha, could you give me an appointment when you're through with those tablets? Josh, I say, it says on the package do not chew, do not crunch, let dissolve slowly in mouth. And then I add, in case of fire, break glass.

I do not know why I said that, I do not know why I say most things.

Yours, half-way to the nut house,

Martha

Dear Mary

When you first wrote that Bobby-Joe was going, I thought you meant back to the Lone Star State, there to do what a man must do, whatever that is, but now you say not at all, he's out on his earhole on the grey paving stones of Sebastopol Terrace, never to darken the door of Number 2 again because you and Mo took a democratic vote, two to one against, and gave him the shove. And all because the poor Texan lad didn't do his share of the housework.

What house? What work? I don't wish to be gratuitously rude but I'd never have guessed that you and Mo were squat-proud. Last time I visited, there was this cucumber lying under the kitchen table so covered in mould it looked like a woolly cactus and I said to Mo why is there a mouldy cucumber lying under your kitchen table and she said because if she picked it up she'd be making a commitment to domesticity. And this is the lady who minds about Bobby-Joe not taking turns doing the washing-up? Has it occurred to her that he might not be able to locate the sink? It took me half an hour to twig that all those interesting fungi in the corner had dishes underneath and the new variety of Venus Fly Trap was actually your communal clettering stick.

I mean, let's face it, your place looks like a giant rat had run amok and gnawed its way through everything in sight. Unless I'd seen it with my own eyes, I'd never have believed that chairs and tables so chewed up could actually remain standing on all three legs. And you may think you've got some sort of order in there but, take it from me, not everyone searching for a toilet roll would necessarily look in the oven and not everyone could guess that the logical niche for sprouting beans is in the cistern.

So why should you both suddenly decide the wretched B-J isn't pulling his weight and dump him? You said yourself he was ace on the guitar and surely he played a bit role in the success of your Orgasmic Therapy course? Can't you find it in your heart to put up with *anything* in the name of love? When I think of what I endure day after day, year after year, screech screech of soap opera strings, all I can say is you're a hard woman, Mary. And if so, why am I sitting here in my cosy nest with my cosy man, cukes neatly stacked in the veggie rack, going green at the edges with envy? I cannot imagine.

Never mind, holsville is nearly here. Actually, I hadn't realized it was nearly here until yesterday evening, when I heard Josh say on the phone to his sec, the doomy Cassandra, that, yes, we were off in August to our little place in France. Then I knew it was the tent again, up the Dordogne. I wonder if Josh is aware he's had a baby since last year? Probably not.

Jane, interrogated as to her holiday plans, said wild horses wouldn't drag her to a canvas tip in Frogland; Ben threw himself about at the thought and produced a series of revolting noises but can I be sure they won't come? I doubt it. Plans, nevertheless, are afoot. Josh, for instance, is deep in the Michelin. Head stuck in the little red book, he reads out things like "Cheval Blanc, Specialité; brochettes de coquilles d'estragon, turbot beurre blanc, sole braisée au Noilly, vins Muscadet" and says, 'What about that Martha? Eh, Martha? What's for dinner, Martha?' — and I have to say bangers and mash.

It's so unfair, Mary. What is all that fuss about these chef minceurs, anyway? I've been cooking minceur forever, and who comes along and awards me four stars for my amazing innovations in ze kitchen? No one. Discrimination again.

All the real cooking goes on in homes, done by women — men just come in at the top of the pyramid wearing silly hats and call themselves maitres de cuisine because they've managed to make something edible out of two gallons of double cream, a haunch of venison and three bottles of brandy. Big deal. Whereas we women can produce a meal for eight out of six decaying veggies, a cube of Oxo and a pound of stale biscuits, which is what I call cooking. Besides, chefs don't have to put up with husbands pigging it and then moaning about their weight.

Last time Josh complained about his, I told him I knew a sure-fire way he could lose 20lb overnight and he said how and I said I could cut his legs off. Then he'd be the teeny toast of the town, like Toulouse Lautrec. I was feeling sore at the time, as it happened. You know that long boring saga I told you two weeks ago about how my shawl got its fringe caught in everything at that party?

Believe it or not, at the supermarket Saturday I bent down to gather up some tins on a low shelf and got my earring entangled in the hair of a small Chinese boy. I had to stay bent over him for ages in the most humiliating way, thinking I'd never heard of anyone who had to be medically severed from a Chinese child except, perhaps, a Chinese mother. What have I done to deserve such punishment?

Coming home, flushed from slaving over a hot Chinese child, I blew off to Josh about how I *must* get a job and save myself from all this. A job? he said. Did I realize, he said, that there were now 2.6 million unemployed and you, Martha, wish to add to that number? *Five* million, I said, sharpish. Five million and one counting me. I'm one of M. Thatcher's fudged statistics, remember? I *want* a job, there aren't any jobs, so I'm forced to wear a hat saying Housewife.

Perhaps, said Josh, you could take a course in Advanced Knitting.

Yours, with the needles out,

Martha

Tai chi chuan

Dear Mary

Are you at all cognizant of what the likes of you and Mo have done, with your Women's Liberationism? Are you aware that you've taken as nice a bunch of modest, sensibly brogued ladies as ever lay back and thought of England and turned them into a monstrous regiment of dirty old women? Transformed them into leering harridans in grubby macs who hang around street corners whistling at anything in trousers that innocently skips by? I've a good mind to shop you to Mrs W so she can stick you in the dock with the Romans, where you belong.

OK. Scratch that. Cancel it, wipe the machine, file it in the wpb. The fact is, I'm in a very distressed state about Ben. You haven't seen him since he was normal. He is now a Brobdingnagian giant. What with jack-knifing down to say googly-goo to one son no higher than my knee-caps and then arching in an S-bend to have a quick word with the other before his head vanishes for ever into deep space, I've got a permanent slippery disc. And if I say so myself, Ben looks terrible. His feet alone take several minutes to enter a room and that a human back-bone can support so many dangling appendages without collapsing like a pack of vertebrae is one of the minor miracles of ergonomics.

Besides that, he's got so many spots it takes a magnifying glass to see the boy in between. Ben flatly denies this. What spots? he says. You're always going on about my spots when I haven't had any for years. Then he asks for a pound to buy Oxy-5, for his spots. What spots? I say. You haven't had any spots for years, right? A cheap victory, I grant you, but I'm not one to look a gift horse in the mouth, can't afford to.

Anyway, yesterday the great lump says he's going out. Where? I say. Out, he says. I cherish these intimate conversations. Then it leaks out he's got a girlfriend. I am genuinely pleased. Fancy that, then, our Ben with a rosy-cheeked damsel, all braces and bunches, sweet sixteens both and never been kissed.

Upon which, Ben announces that said damsel is thirty-five. Thirty-*five*? *Thirty-five*? Mum, says Ben, your record's stuck. But Ben, I say, you're *sixteen*. *So*? says Ben. You an ageist, Mum or something? But Ben, I say, what on earth does a thirty-five-year-old woman want with *you*? And do you know, Mary, the twit gives a sickening smirk, adjusts his shoulder bones in the hall mirror, clicks his fingers at his reflection, and erupts out the front door squawking like a rooster. Leaving me, his mother, 38, alone and palely loitering. Is there such a thing as senile nymphomentia? How does she treat him, what does she say? Ben, you wash your hands before you come to bed, hear me? And just look at those nails. Will you for Pete's sake stand still while I talk to you, stop fidgeting, and *please* turn that music down before my eardrums puncture. Is that any sort of prelude to life's tenderest moments? The woman must be round the twist.

There I was, with the birds-and-bees all planned, ready for Ben's first whisper of romance. A motherly man-to-man chat about responsibilities and courtesy to the opposite sex and always using the necessaries. And now I'm locked in combat with a female pederast. It's too much. How am I supposed to mother an innocent babe and a sex-crazed teenage clown, all at the same time? Mornings spent sticking Heinz Chicken Dinner in a small mouth, one for Mummy, down the little red lane, evenings spent embroiled in a May to September saga of mismatched lust. No one woman can bridge such gulfs.

Josh is no use. He coarsened before my eyes when told and clapped Ben on the back for the first time since he learned his five times tables. I'm going to write to Ben's father and make him *do* something. At least it'll tear him away from his rotten *Flasher's Guide to Feminism*. Did I tell you he's sent the first chapter to Josh? Haw haw, says Josh, laughing immoderately, you must have a read, Martha. Thanks, but no thanks, I said. As it happens, I did catch a glimpse. The first page: How to Seduce a Feminist. Tell her, 'Oh, Ms Croggs, if you'd only put your hair in a bun and wear glasses, you'd be beautiful.' Vulgar trash and typical of my ex.

In the midst of these upsets my friend Lorna, the autopsy technician, appeared and said why didn't I come with her that evening and have my feet massaged by this marvellous man who could solve all my problems by rummaging round my insteps. So I went and he stuck his fingers quite painfully into my big toe and when I said ouch he told me that showed I was a deeply sensitive and misunderstood person, which is

so true, Mary. He also said I was pitifully exposed to other people's feelings and must wear a black cummerbund round my middle to protect myself from emotional vibrations that make martyrs of generous and vulnerable souls like myself. He guessed my star sign, too, or the one I would have had if I hadn't been in such a hurry to get away from Mother. The man is clearly psychic and the first for a long time to see into the real me. Such an aesthetic demeanour. Such compelling eyes. Such strong yet gentle hands.

Yours, strangely moved,

Martha

Dear Mary

Got about five minutes to write this before Josh, me and the baby depart for our place in France, ie *le tente*. Does tente mean tent? Probably not. In my experience, the more the French word is like the English the more it's different and usually rude. Have we got an *entente cordiale* at the moment? I can't remember if we've just stopped fighting about lamb or just started fighting about fish. I shall scrape the GB off the car on the other side, just in case. Do not wish to be pursued by enraged froggies down the N1.

Over the weekend Josh (generous to a fault? Oiling up the ladder?) announced he'd swopped Department hols with this VIP called Tinkerton-Smith because T-S and wife have marital problems and can't get away. I've met the Tinkerton-Smiths. They look like two rubber balls with specs on, it's a miracle they manage to have sex without bouncing. Anyway, I was furious. *We're* the ones who'll have marital problems, I said, if you think I'm going to pack for three and organize two others plus cats, goldfish and white mice, all in two days. Oh I told him, Mary. Out of the question, I said. Quite impossible. *Pas de chance, oubliez-le* and so on. I was adamant.

So we're off. Ben's gone already, on this morning's train to Mousehole and his Dad. He protested like mad about leaving his fish, his mice and his girlfriend, in that order, but there's a silver lining to every cloud – surely he'll meet a nice Cornish girl nearer his age, like thirty, instead of that predatory crone he's taken up with? Tom was none too pleased when I phoned but I didn't give him a chance to talk. I said Tom, your son arrives 1.45 pm, Penzance, today. His name's Ben, he's wearing an orange rucksack, you can't miss him. And I slammed the phone down on the rising rumbles from the other end. That was the bit I enjoyed. Ben can be guaranteed to sabotage *The Flasher's Guide*, at least for a while.

Jane was more of a problem. She mooned about complaining of being exploited, having to stay in the rotten house to feed rotten rodents. I'd told her she could have a girl friend in or go to her Grandmother's and Mrs Next-Door would come in to feed the beasts but Jane said she didn't have girl friends and mooned some more. Then, yesterday evening, she comes in with this stunning young man. I mean *stunning*, Mary. Well over six foot, marigold hair, cornelian eyes and medallions all over amazing pectorals. As I got up off the floor, Jane said this is Rover, Ma, a mate of mine. He'll stay for the month. So will I, I said. No, of *course* I didn't. I said Jane, look Jane, hullo Rover, look Rover, you must understand. I can't leave you both in the house, alone together. Why ever not? said Jane staring. Well, Jane, you're a girl and Rover is a man. You . . . I . . . it wouldn't do.

I dare say I came over a mite coy then, blinking and twittering and fluttering, while they both stood there and gazed at me, their eyes four blank discs of incomprehension. What? said Jane. Pardon? said Rover. It dawned on me then that neither Jane nor Rover would recognize sex if it fell on top of them in the dark. Between the two of them, they've obviously finished off the permissive society and buried it in a pauper's grave so they might just as well fill up the resulting free time scattering goldfish food on goldfish and mice food on mice. So I said, oh very well. Besides, in my sad experience, men who look like Rover look only at their mothers.

My mother, of course, popped up by popular demand to do her evergreen music-hall turn, the one with the refrain that goes 'what if.' What if, says Mother, Jane falls over the cat, breaks every limb and starves to death because Rover isn't there because Rover's mother's died and he's had to go to Buenos Aires for her funeral? What if ten thousand unemployed youths, brains bleached by the peroxide they put on their hair, riot in our back garden? What if a mad axeman escapes from Broadmoor, thumbs a lift to our street corner, breaks in and rapes Jane who jumps out of the front window? Not to mention the one about what if Rover or the longer one about Ben (falls out of train, fractures skull, gets amnesia and is never seen again). What would you do *then*, Martha? You'd never forgive yourself, Martha. Oh how we all clapped. This one will run and run.

One good thing, though – I'll miss the Wedding. What a happy deliverance from the Royal Charade! I've no wish at all to sit and watch while one poor little girl, the same age as our Jane, is sentenced to a life-time of flatties. And I know I can rely on you and Mo to give me no details whatsoever of the Wedding Dress. You haven't got a telly, anyway, have you? Mind you, I may be forced to watch in France, somewhere. You know how besotted the Continentals are about our Royals and I wouldn't want to be boorish, if anyone insisted. When in Rome, I always say.

And as Mrs Next-Door always says, you don't go on holiday to do what you *want,* do you, dear?

Yours, with the seat-belts clunked and clicked,

Martha

Dear Mary

Driven 1000 kms through deepest France, baby pogo-ing on lap, shrieking in earhole, whacking in face. Arrive camp shaking wreck, bruised neck to knees, sporting black eye, to be greeted by Hooray Henry in next tent who takes butcher's at me, says ho ho ho ho, who's on her honeymoon then, eh what? Did not drive 1000 kms to squat cheek by jowl with dread GB hearty sniggering about sex. *Sex imposs.* anyway. Baby's nose just reaches top of canvas cot, from whence he regards us all night long with unblinking stare.

Just glimpsed Josh's card to sec. Says 'Wish you were her'. Is this sloppy spelling or end of marriage?

Votre, sans un trace de ooh la la,

Martha

Dear Mary

Due to hitherto undetected EEC apricot mountain, baby has runs – ie baby sits, I run. Result: this postcard written under low cloud formed by fall-out from nappies incinerating in some foreign field that is forever England. Elsewhere, Old Sol works overtime. Yesterday, braving Josh's mutters, I appear topless on river beach. One glance at forgotten globes & baby goes into thirst-maddened-desert-castaway-crawling-to-wards-mirage-of-drinking-fountain number. V. embarrassing. Have to peel him forcibly off intimate anatomy to chorus of *dommages* from French mamans on brink of shopping me to Dordogne branch of NSPCC.

Votre, la belle dame sans merci,

Martha

Dear Mary

These past 24 hours have brought our little family remarkably close. Mainly because if we so much as touch the outside canvas, rain pours in. Il pleut, Mary, comme chats et chiens. Gigantic Citroen parked opposite to view (I thought) les foreign misérables, turns out to be Josh's dear old college chum Yves de Tiswas, come to convey us to his maison de campagne, complete with brocantes and meubles traditionelles anglaises (expensive bum-numbing wooden benches). Yves has a maid, too, an honest-to-goodness becapped, befrilled, be-black-stockinged maid. Josh now in deep sulk. He's worked his guts out, voted EEC since Heath was young, so how come Yves, a fool if ever there was one and lazy to boot, not to say un pouffe from way back, is rolling in francs? But Josh, I said, I thought he was your *friend*. What's that got to do with it? says Josh, enragé. Les hommes, quelle mystère ils sont.

   Votre, wishing I was there,

Martha

Josh thinking about Yves....

Dear Mary

Am exstatically happy – Ekstatically happy? Something not quite right there but no Concise Oxford handy so who cares. Sun hot, wine cold, only blot on horizon pack-up time rapidly approaching. Baby brown as chip off Old Potato. Said to Old Potato, why can't we always live in tent, just you and me? OP replied 'And Ben and Jane and the baby AND your mother and let's not forget Studs.' Heart sank. Didn't know he knew about Studs, not that anything to know. Had flashback about day Josh came home early, found Studs carving leftover roast. Realize now any woman caught in flagrante with man carving husband's roast, worse than adulteress.

Yours attrappée bang to rights,

Martha

Dear Mary

Sorry no letter last week, just arrived home zonked out. Missed road, missed boat, nearly missed England. Bad trip. Hey, wait a minute, I'm not writing postcards any more. I can expand out of the glottal stops, stick in the odd pronoun, dust off an adjective or two, get into expressing myself full frontally again. Not that there's a whole lot to express. My tan has faded to what we housewives call dirty and the first faint spots of autumn have broken out across the baby's bum. Oh to be in la Dordogne, now that London's here. Well, all good things must come to an end.

Anyway, I got your card and I'm glad you're home, too. No lolling about in the ultra-violet for you, I see. No sooner do I turn my back than you scamper off to yet another Summer School. What was it, this time? The Experiential Ethos of the Feminine Principle, Logic or Myth? Something like that.

Honestly, sometimes I wonder about Wales. It was Wales you were in, wasn't it? Like California, when they tipped Britain on its side all the nuts rolled into Wales. Our nuts, not theirs. First they got hordes of hippies cantering across the Severn Bridge in the Sixties, kneedeep in cowbells, stiff with joss and Acapulco Gold, hellbent on filling in the Welsh valley with rotting plastic mattresses and throttling the natives with their awful macrame. And the moment they'd gone, in came the next wave, religious nuts this time, complete with woodsy altars to replace the nice, dull Welsh chapels. Daughters of the Moon. Kiddywinks of God. Church of Christ, Dentist. All that. What must God have felt, peering through the clouds (the Welsh do a nice line in clouds) and seeing all those loony little faces raised to Him, chanting mantras and arranging their limbs in inscrutable Eastern positions? A bit like the last of the Raj, I shouldn't wonder.

And now they're shuddering under the latest wave – batty Self-Improvers who rush over with their rucksacks and unspeakable sleeping bags to register for weekends in Ego Expansion and Ancient Kurdish Skipping Rhymes. Whenever you hear of a new group that's into anything light years away from useful, where are they doing it? Wales is where. Not surprisingly, they make bonfires of our cottages. I could find it in my heart to light a match or two myself. Yes, I know all that sounds the teeniest bit Fascistic and I know you'll think I'm being hostile but it's not meant that way. I am trying to talk about you first, like it says in those books about how to win friends. Do not push yourself, it warns in Chapter One. Listen to others' problems, ask them about themselves, learn to be a listener. Well, you've had your innings. It's all me from now on.

I won't say the place was a mess when we got home because it wasn't too bad. Jane had fought back the encroaching jungle in at least the kitchen, the bathroom, and our bedroom but she'd given up on the sitting room. Breaking in, I knew suddenly how Howard Carter must have felt, discovering King Tut's tomb. The very atmosphere was heavy with times past. Two vases of roses were almost perfectly preserved though, alas, as the door creaked open and fresh air rushed in, they crumbled into dust before my eyes. And, believe it or not, I found intricately emblazoned beer cans containing the actual fag-ends, left exactly as they were by the long-gone folk of yore. There were even the yellowed shards of Sunday papers lying open on the floor, where the last inhabitants had dropped them before the vault slammed shut. It was so moving, Mary, it brought tears to my eyes.

Ben had returned a week earlier, jaded by the highlife of Mousehole. He seems to have spent the time in what he calls his bed, actually a cage he's constructed of bookshelves cunningly interwoven with white mice, a few goldfish and two pots of ivy expanded into a trellis of greenery between him and the outside world. Within, he can be dimly perceived, a shy gorilla amongst forest leaves, munching through comics like *National Lampoon*, that disgusting American mag Tom saw fit to give him last birthday. How's Dad? I said. OK, he said. What did you do? I said. Nothing, he said. Sometimes I wonder will I ever stem the flood?

Josh, having put in an appearance at the office, stormed home very put out. Someone had moved his desk. They *had*. Stuck it under the window instead of sideways to the door and pinched his swivel chair. Poor lamb. Really, Mary, I don't know how some men bear their lot, do you? Just imagine coming home and finding you have to face due South instead of North, as was. Enough to snap the stoutest nerve. I said to Josh, I don't see you have any option but to resign. Otherwise, what shred of dignity have they left you? I mean, if people think they can push you around like that, next time you're away you might find you'd made a whole 180 degree turn, without a word of authorization or a single signed slip. And after that, anything might happen – you could end up press-ganged into the SDP. Do you know, the way my husband looks at me sometimes, I don't think he even *likes* me.

Yours, home and wet,

Martha

'Testify!' —

The church of Christ, Dentist.

Dear Mary

I don't know what to do about Rover. Here it is, September, and he shows no signs of leaving, nor does a ripple of anxiety disturb the delightful harmony of his brow. Jane says we can't come home from foreign parts whenever it suits us and chuck him out on the street and Rover stands like a block of polished steel and says uh-huh. When it *suits* us? I said. The way I feel now, Rover's welcome to move in with Josh and I'll chuck *myself* out on the street, if not the window. I believe this is what's called the post-hols blues.

I suppose, Mary, you couldn't put him up at Sebastopol Terrace, could you? Haven't you an odd cupboard free, now that Bobby-Joe has gone? Rover doesn't seem to have any direct connection with London, like work or friends or the theatre – have you noticed how ex-Londoners always say, of course, I *do* miss the theatre when they've never even seen *The Mousetrap*? It's true Rover doesn't do very much except look in the mirror and twitch his muscles but you can't blame him for that, seeing as how he's so ornamental. You could pretend he was a large and exotic parrot you'd bought to brighten up the home, albeit a bird daft as two planks who can only say uh-huh.

I wouldn't mind having him all that much but Josh would and he's under the illusion that Rover's already gone, anyway. He thinks he comes in the evening to see Jane but he doesn't know he sneaks upstairs after banging the front door hard like I told him to. All he's faintly concerned with is Jane's purity – is she saving herself for a husband? Whereas I know Rover's no threat – he's saving himself for himself. Do write and tell me if you can house him because I can't go on much longer concealing him in the attic like Mr Rochester's mad wife. Yesterday, him and Josh nearly collided on the way to the bathroom and I got so nervous I ate a whole treacle tart.

Ben went out yesterday and came back with the woman he calls his old lady and no wonder. You remember his aged amour, the 35-year-old cradlesnatcher? It was her and, much as I hate to admit it, she's really rather nice, even if she is only two years younger than me. She's called Wendy. Not, I grant you, a name that reverberates in the soul. No one is going to sing Wendy, Wendy, the most wonderful name in the world, but it suits her and she's *very* maternal. She picked up the baby right away and dandled him the whole time we were chatting. Ben got bored and went off to watch the Muppets and we got on with our girl-talk. Mind you, I kept an eye peeled as she left in case she showed signs of transferring her affection from Ben to the baby and tried to smuggle him out. Come to think of it, she'd make a handy baby-sitter.

It's so odd, the way things work. For hundreds of years, fathers have been giving away daughters to men their own age, as if they were passing them on to another father, in most ways, they were. But it should be the other way round, shouldn't it? Boys are so much more childish than girls. Jane could cope with practically everything when she was 12 but it still takes Ben about half-an-hour to tie his shoe laces. Perhaps, between me and Wendy we can start a whole new matriarchal trend. I can quite see myself walking up the aisle, Ben's hand gripped firmly in mine (stop it now or Mummy will smack), and depositing it in Wendy's capable grasp at the altar, knowing I can trust her to see that he brushes his teeth properly, up and down, eats plenty of green veggies, and has a bath at least once a week including back of neck.

She's a good thrifty housewife, too. Told me how she makes her own sheets and you *know* the price of sheets. Well, you should know. The only trouble is, talking about sheets makes me think of her and Ben lying under them. Yuk. I feel, now, I ought to get in touch with Wendy's mother, to warn her about my son. She lives in Bournemouth. I happen to know that interesting fact because Wendy said she had to visit her and Ben said oh *why* and Wendy said she is 70, you know, and Ben said well, you'd better run, then. He goes back to school next week. Thank heaven.

I got your letter explaining about your summer course in the Ethos of the Feminine Principle, Logic or Myth, and I say unto you it's Myth. Look, it sounds fine, arguing that if men cooked and women engineered, the battle of the sexes would grind to a halt but that's not my experience. When – *when* – Josh cooks, the merest turn of a wooden spoon becomes the essence of masculinity. His bechamel stirs him to the very peaks of machoism and if he produces even the tiredestlooking cake he reckons he's John Wayne, jingling spurs, funny walk, drawl, the lot. If ah'd known you was comin', ah'd of baked a cake, baby. Whereas Josh comes upon me repairing the boiler with a spanner I happen to have painted a face on, for no reason whatsoever, and he laughs tenderly like men do when they're thinking how deeply, lovably, and transparently inferior women actually are. And I titter back.

Yours, stuck in a gender trap,

Martha

← Wendy

Dear Mary

I wrote to ask if you could put Rover up at Sebastopol Terrace and you write back and say you can't 'on account of the CND'. What does that mean? Josh, who's taken a quite unaccountable dislike to poor Rove, says you've discovered what he's known all along, Rove's a human neutron bomb – he destroys people, not property. Which is very mean of Josh and also inaccurate, as he would know if I'd ever let him see the gouged-out floorboards in Ben's room where Rover drops his dumb-bells from on high.

The only connection I can imagine is that you've got CNDers staying while they're on some march but, in that case, they'd be classified as itinerants or nomads or something and Rove could come when they've passed on. Unless you're on some permanent CND shuttle service between Land's End and Chancellor Schmidt?

Yes I know. I sound irritable and I am. Ben is having the longest school holidays in the history of education. Every day he makes noises like he's going off, he disappears, I breathe a sigh of relief and abracadabra, he's back again. Just registering, he says, waving various bits of blank paper. Really, I could almost suspect the school didn't want him, which is weird. Well, weirdish.

Yesterday, he came in, cleared his throat and said Mum, I've made a decision. My heart leapt up. He's taking French, I thought. He's really going to work hard. He's decided he's going to be a doctor. Wrong again. Mum, says Ben, I've decided what I want for Christmas. Christmas. Oh good, Ben I said. What a relief to us all. Wait till I tell Father Christmas, he *will* be pleased.

Besides Ben, there is the baby, once so sweet and lovable, now a home-breaker. Could the Martians have whipped the real infant away and left us with a wind-up intergalactic spy? When I put him down on the floor, he crawls off at top speed like one of those horrid mechanical toys that used to frighten me so when I was a kid. Mary, I swear he *whirrs*.

Jane stands there yelling do something, Mum, it's coming at me, don't let it get in my room. Also, he's taken to emitting unearthly shrieks. All of a sudden the mechanics fail, the limbs come to a grinding halt, a hole appears in the centre of the face and out of it comes a series of eardrum-perforating screams, as if he were permanently attached to a maddened wasp.

What really unnerves me is, he watches me while he's shrieking and his face is perfectly blank and sort of inwardly absorbed, as if he were passing on some message to an invisible walkie-talkie. Agent PZ254 calling Mars. OK, Mars. Mission accomplished. Multiparous Terran Female cracking up. What's more, there's Josh complaining all the time that he's aware food prices have gone up and he knows there's inflation but my food bills are ridiculous. Josh, I want to say, they're not ridiculous, they're Rover, but I daren't. Josh, hit in the pocket, is not a pretty sight.

Worse, I fear Jane may be falling in love with Rover. She kicks him a lot, jumps out on him from corners bellowing like that Japanese in the Pink Panther films and rolls her eyes heavenwards whenever he speaks, grunting Jeez.

I wish I could be philosophical about it all and think 'this, too, will pass' but that only reminds me so will I, and soon, if this goes on. You, Mary, who communicate only with adults, can have little idea what it's like to be locked for life in the monkeys' cage at the zoo. Ever so entertaining if you're on the outside, pushing snacks through the bars and looking forward to a nice cup of tea in a peaceful kitchen. Another thing altogether to find, when the visitors go and the keepers switch the lights off, that you're banged up in the chimps' tea party.

My only relief this week has been Lorna, my friend across the road. I'm not surprised she's a mortician technician, suits her down to the ground, ho ho. Last week they buried the grumpy old boy who ran the basket shop in the high street. Oh dear, I mumbled hypocritically, his poor family. Yeah, said Lorna, grief-stricken as newts they were.

Then she goes on about a girl she was on holiday with, the one with the wavy copper hair and emerald eyes and ugly. Apparently the kiddies on the beach had flocked around her. She's obviously got a magnetism for kiddies, I said. They're drawn to her. No they're not, said Lorna, they just wanted an eyeful of the holes in her cossie. As for Lorna's friend's husband, all she'd say about him was he had breasts the same shape as his wife's. Honestly, Lorna's inner life must look a bit like Ben's goldfish bowl, all green and murky and full of dark shapes.

Josh is no help. When I try and discuss Ben with him, he raises his face towards me and his eyes close, just like a sleepy-doll. I mean, I know Ben isn't his son but you'd think he'd take an interest for my sake. Last week I was moaning on about the lad and this time Josh didn't even raise his face. Look, I said, do you realize that sometimes teenage boys are really worried about some things, really disturbed, and their parents never bother and then, out of the blue, they kill themselves? He'll grow out of it, said Josh vaguely, it's only a phase. You can't grow out of death, I said. Hanging may do wonders for venison, but it is no maturing process for human beings. He wasn't listening.

About the only thing that gets through to him at the moment is the baby's shrieks. Is that why the baby shrieks? Clever thing.

Yours, deaf-aid off,

Martha

16 September

Dear Mary

Josh entered the house at seven pip emma yesterday, bounced off Rover's pectorals in the hall, fell over Ben's bike in the kitchen, took the full blast of the baby in mid-aria, poured himself the sludge at the bottom of the holiday Pernod, said here's to the ladies bless 'em and *smiled* at me – I know he's smiling when the front of his hair moves. Ye gods and fishes, I thought, Maggie's made him Sir Josh. But no. Martha, he said, making toasting gestures at me, good news for you. The Boss has decided to stand for Parliament and I'm behind her one hundred percent so don't ever say again that I'm against your women's lib.

Well. For a moment there I thought the floor and I were about to come together. A frightful pain shot through my heart and buried itself in the region of my spleen. Ms Boss, MP? Just twenty-four hours ago I'd expressed a desire to attend my very small women's group for a very short time and Josh had come on like I planned to desert him for a career in Hollywood. He had, he protested, *papers* to go through and how could a man go through *papers* with a baby at his feet making noises like it was about to take off for Saturn? So I didn't go. And now we have Irene, already at the pinnacle of one male edifice, plotting to scale yet another with the one hundred percent support of my spouse. Furthermore, a spouse who's acting as if she's some sort of Joan of Arc for her pains. And the two of them couldn't blow their own noses without help from ancillary staff.

So there I am in an upright swoon, pinned to my chair by a ton-weight of envy and resentment and a headache coming on fast, when who should appear but the Maid of Orleans herself, clad in shining white Vanderbilt coveralls (I myself am modishly got up in Sixties bell-bottoms and some parts of a sweater Jane got tired of knitting). And Mary, the woman is iridescent. Nostrils aflare with the scent of power, face flushed across to the ears with naked ambition. She's fresh from some boat trip of women egging each other on to Westminster and she looks like the Bride of Dracula after a boozy weekend. Even the baby feels upstaged and cuts out suddenly on a high note.

And what does Josh, Knight-at-Arms, do? Goes across to the cupboard, takes out the bottle of champagne he's set aside for some intimate marital occasion like the day Mother kicks the bucket, pops the cork and pours froth all over the place while our foetal MP smiles and smiles. One of these days, that woman will smile me to death. Then, downing her champers, Irene sails over to me, puts one exquisitely manicured hand on my dish-pan appendages, looks moistly into my eyes and says Martha dear, I hope we can all rise to the challenge, look beyond mere Party prejudice and vote for me. We girls must stick together, mustn't we?

If I'd had the breadknife handy, I'd have drawn it across both our throats. And I trust, Mary, you're not thinking good for Irene, we need more women in Parliament because, if you are, don't bother to put a 14p stamp on it. Irene MP would do women like me about as much good as the rhythm method. Not only will she forget the ordinary woman's lot – she never knew it. She'll waltz about the corridors of power in her £300 Jean Muir number with a bodyguard of masseurs and coiffeurs plucking at her and appear night and day on telly to lecture such as me on the sanctity of marriage and the marvels of motherhood.

I tell you, that woman is the Marie Antoinette of our time, she even has a weeny thatched cotty in the Cotswolds where she goes and pats sheep. Any minute now, she'll be saying let them eat Textured Vegetable Protein. You're thinking she resembles Mrs T? Matey, she makes that lady look like Marx in drag. At least Maggie has momentarily experienced childbirth even if it was two for the labour of one and into boarding school before they could call her Mother, whereas Ms Doss has done nothing more female than stick her feet in stacked heels. Why in heaven's name should I support a person just because it wears skirts? So does King Khalid and he's in line for no feminist prizes.

Don't you *want* women in Parliament to defend your interests? said Josh, in bed that night. Yah boo sucks, I sobbed. And then, you know what? He puts his arm around me, gives me a little squeeze and says listen, Martha, let me spell it out. If Irene gets to Parliament, who gets to be Boss? D'you see, little Martha? D'you see why I'm behind her?

There's men for you, Mary, deceivers all. Vipers in the grass, snakes in the woodpile, leaders up the garden path and leavers at the altar. Poor Irene, poor silly dear, how's she going to manage in politics if she can't tell the difference between a pat on the back and a knife between the ribs? We girls must stick together.

Yours in sisterly solidarity,

Martha

Dear Mary

Amazed to hear that you and Mo were on that Women-for-Parliament cruise, too, and actually met Irene face to face. Or would have, as you say, if the ten tons of make-up she was wearing hadn't prevented her lifting said face above the Plimsoll line. Mean remarks like that, Mary, make me realize you are not so much a Sister, more a bosom friend. I hate to be brutally frank in return but I must tell you I'm not truly convinced, even so, that you and Mo are likely to lead me, your humble womb-defined female voter, much further along the path to paradise than Irene.

Does life as it is lived up Sebastopol Terrace say a whole lot more to me than Ms Boss's division-bell penthouse and Cotswold cotty? Answer, not a syllable. I won't go on about Motherhood again because I promise you I don't really count giving birth as among the outstanding qualifications for women MPs but is my choice of a life-enhancing economic policy stuck between Irene's Brylcreemed commodity-brokers overcharging on hoarded Third World coffee and your strategy of nicking Sainsbury's Instant whenever the whim strikes? I dare say you both succeed in redistributing some wealth but not, I'd like to point out, in my direction.

This analysis may be lacking in depth. We housewives find it practically impossible to obtain four minutes' quiet in which to formulate abstract thought. During the past half-hour, for instance, Ben has been padding up and down behind my left ear muttering tiddley pom tiddley pom tiddley pom, over and over. Ben, I finally said to him, other boys of your age do not spend their days saying tiddley pom over and over in this ridiculous fashion. Furthermore, Lorna's son, who is exactly your age, told me yesterday a great many interesting facts about the chemical that makes oak apples into oak apples and I must say (I added, meanly) I rather wished *he* was my son. Mary, all that boy did was look vaguely in my direction and say and was he? Was he? I said. Ben, what d'you mean, *was* he? Of course he wasn't, you idiot. He's *Lorna's* son. I mean, Alice in Wonderland, Mary.

Do you wonder I can't concentrate under these circumstances?

That sort of thing happens all the time with Ben. The other day we went and picnicked by the Thames, under a tree with a boat tied to it. Ben sat in the boat and said Mum, why have they tied that tree to this boat? They haven't, I said. They've tied the boat to the tree. How do you know? he said. Perhaps they think the tree might get stolen. You see? Is there such a thing as dyslexia of the entire personality and, if so, what's the cure? In my more optimistic moments (last one, June 5, 1978) I put Ben's behaviour down to what that nice Mr de Bono calls lateral thinking and only crude and ignorant people call barmy.

Be that as it may, such goings-on make abstract political ideas hard to come by and forces me to realize the appeal of the SDP who will do it all for us, and nicely, because they are nice people and kindly ignore the silly things folk like me say, such as get rid of nuclear missiles and so on, because they know we don't know what we're saying. Which, remembering the CND chums you've got snoozing on your floorboards, brings me back to the pressing problem of how to kick out Rover. He, along with Jane, is now manifesting all the natural gaiety of a vulture. When I make noises like he's got to go, Jane says he's a squatter and has squatters' rights and I say, quick as a flash, no he hasn't because we all share the same loo. That is legally correct, isn't it? So Jane says that one won't work because Rover doesn't use our loo because he's the sort of person that can't use other people's loos. What on earth does he *do* then? I said crossly. Goes at his auntie's down the road, she said. Well, can't he take a bit more than his kidneys to his auntie's? I said. No, said Jane, she's only got a bed-sit.

Really, it's too stupid. Can you imagine me fighting this one out in a court of law? Me: M'lud, the accused is squatting. Rover: M'lud, I'm not squatting, I pee at my auntie's. How did I get *into* this? Tell you what, Mary, this is the sort of complicated trivia that make up real MPs' lives. If you and Mo come up with a solution to Rover's floating kidneys, you'll have my vote. I'll put it to Irene, too, and may the best woman win.

Yours, ballot paper poised,

Martha

Jane
defending
the sort of
person who
can't use
other people's
loos

Dear Mary

Last week (reason why I didn't write) I got these agonizing pains, at least seven of them. My gums swelled up all along the molars, the glands under my chin felt like loose ball-bearings, my stomach took off for foreign parts, with only the occasional letter home, and the parts of me left behind got fed into a concrete mixer. Josh, I said. Do you ever get a pain so painful that if it went on longer than a quarter of a second, your nails would fall out? The flickery sort of pain, Josh, the kind that flashes up the soles of your feet, tunnels through your ribcage, streaks across your neck and explodes out of your left ear? The kind that makes you think God is skewering you for a celestial shish kebab? No, said Josh. But Josh, I said. Don't you ever get a very *small* pain? Even the teeniest twinge in, say, the third metatarsal from the right or just under your nosebone? No, he said. Sometimes I think I am married to someone not of flesh and blood at all. Sometimes I think they ran up Josh in some laboratory, wodged him together out of a strange, thick substance, like pressed-felt carpet tiles.

I couldn't even call the doctor, due to the fact that Kev is back and stripping the wallpaper from the bedroom wall. You remember Kev, who kept seeing the Royal Family on our ceiling? Marf, he said when he arrived at the door. They give me ESP in that place and I'm cured. Now he only sees Princess Anne's baby and that only occasionally, in the odd bit of wallpaper. Which, considering he saw the Queen, the Duke, Princesses M and A and Princes C, A and E before, is pretty well a cure by any standards. So Kev's large as life again, showering plaster down on the two of us, making me look like a long-dead corpse. If the doctor did come, he'd only diagnose lead poisoning or some other variation on what might be called a Decorational Disease.

Poor Jane had to cope with the baby because she's still on holiday till next week. I say 'poor Jane' but, actually, she'd got herself perfectly organized. She'd dump a bowl of shredded wheat on my tummy at 9 am and then take off, baby and Rover and all, to her friends in this squat. The baby arrived back every evening looking like he'd been forked out of an allotment, like a new potato. He was just one staggering smut. Jane, he's *filthy*, I'd say in shock horror. Yeah, she'd say he is, isn't he? She didn't seem to care at all, she seemed to think that it didn't matter, babies being filthy, because of them being washable and pre-shrunk and permanently-pleated. I got this nasty redundant feeling, especially since the only thing I could see through the grime were the baby's teeth, exposed in a blissful grin.

Why did Doctor Spock never reveal that all babies want in life is squats and filth? I reckon it's a capitalist conspiracy to keep mothers in the home buying 20 different varieties of baby-cleaning products. The advertisers hire troops of evil little gnomes to impersonate kiddies who *like* being washed and eating wholewheat muesli and Marmite, when all the time what really makes them happy is grovelling about in dirt munching old potato peelings.

It's a conspiracy that has put a stone on me. I dare say if I wasn't so fat, I'd feel less pain – obviously, the more there is of you, the more lebensraum germs have to work in. My trouble is, I don't think I'm a teapot, I think I'm a dustbin. I have this overwhelming urge to fill myself with left-overs. Down the little red lane, I say to the baby and the baby says ugh and down my little red lane go the stewed prunes, the pureed spinach, the chicken-and-carrot dinner, the soggy rusks, the chewed banana. *Pour encouragez les autres.* What's more, if anyone ever said to me, Martha, how do you fancy a fry-up of a dried-out pork chop, three cold roast spuds, six limp celery tops and a wedge of mouldy cheese? I'd say not a lot, thanks awfully. But that's what I eat, myself, every time I defrost the fridge. Oh look, world, I say. See what a good, thrifty housewife I am. There's not one left-over in my pantry. It's all neatly packed away on my hips.

Josh pronounced my illness psychosomatic, brought on by refusing to face the fact that I can't get into anything but my bell-bottomed jeans. It's true that nighties are the only garments that flatter me and I suppose you can't be an entirely well person while walking about in nighties. Perhaps I'll marry Kev. His monarchical interests might divert him from marital flab, unless he started seeing Lady Di in the folds of my spare tyre.

Oh, Mary, I've gone on about myself and there's you sunk in gloom because of Mr Benn, and threatening to defect to the SDP so you can ruin *their* vote for a deputy leader. Look at it this way. Isn't it nicer just to dream about a new decor for the Labour Party? When the old wallpaper is actually peeled off, you get horribly choked up with dust and debris and bits of asbestos fluff that set off a terminal respiratory ailment, quite possibly. Sorry. The metaphor is drearily domestic but d'you see what I mean?

Yours, coughing up old flock,

Martha

LOOK....
There it
is again!

— HORRIBLE!

Kev spotting Princess Anne's baby.

Dear Mary

That was some bonfire you set off up here, Thursday. Three am, all's quiet and then brr, brr there's Mo shouting down the phone about Old Bill having got you for breaking into a sex shop. I tell Josh and, half asleep, he explodes. Good grief, he howls, who the hell is this Bill, getting his paramours to steal sex aids in the middle of the night? Can't he effing well resign himself to being effing well impotent like any decent man? Christ's sake, Martha, I know your friends are round the bend but do they have to be raving nymphos to boot? The poor man was all confused, you see, and to add to it, he'd accidentally switched on the bedside radio and some young mother was blethering on about the problems of raising kids in high-rise flats. Problems? bellows Josh. Is it any bloody wonder you women have problems, with half of you yakking all night on the radio and the other half raiding sex shops? If it were up to me, I'd have the whole lot of you put down.

I'm trying to explain to him what Old Bill means and about there being such things, in the twentieth century, as recorded broadcasts when in comes Jane saying it's very nice, she's sure, old people like us having a sex life, but do we have to wake the whole house and in comes Ben yelling is it a fire and we can all climb out the window on his trained ivy and then, to cap it all, the baby lets fly and Mrs Next-Door starts hammering on the wall fit to bust her garters. By the time Friday morning dawns, Josh has served me with six parking tickets and my divorce papers and I'm into my fourth nervous breakdown.

We've picked up the pieces now but, Mary, are sex shops really worth all that hassle? I mean, I take your point about the principle of it all and women not being sex objects and porn fodder and that but it's a funny world that pops you, Mo and Mrs Whitehouse in the same bag. I'm sure Lenin was right, as you say, using any group to further his own aims but, personally, I'd happily sell a gross of tickling sticks rather than go through what I went through that night. What price a sex shop at the end of Sebastopol Terrace when I may never have a sex life again, because of it?

Seriously, though, I am on your side. We keep the Guinness Book of Records in the bathroom and it fell open the other day and inside it was some frightful magazine full of frightful women on some insane gynaecological rampage. Oh Lord, I thought. Not only is Josh short-tempered but he's a hypocrite as well. He wants his respectably wedded spouse to do what these women do for a wage packet I won't see in a month of Sundays. Why doesn't he put his money where his mouth is? Sorry, I'd like to have put that another way. And it turned out not to be Josh at all but something Rover left behind when he took off for his auntie's and all I can say is, I hope his auntie's OK.

But, Mary, I do understand what you meant to do by breaking into that shop. It's true, if the honest citizens of Sebastopol Terrace had seen all those sexy appliances spread over the street when they woke up, they might have joined your cause. Too bad the police managed to tidy it all up before morning and charge you. Of course I'll be a character witness even though, obviously, it'll cost me my marriage and Josh will get custody of the kids and two of them aren't even his and probably their *real* father is a mail-order subscriber to that very sex shop. What a mess.

Mother came over the day after your fiasco and when I told her about it, she approved, which ought to bring you out in a cold sweat. My Mother thinks bananas are pornographic. Goodness knows how I was ever conceived – I'd say my Dad must have swum over her, except he can't swim. When I mentioned the pains I had last week, she said I must have had an episcopal pregnancy. That, Mother, I said, is what the bishop said to the actress but she didn't understand. Most of the time, when I talk, she just stands there shaking her head and saying she's glad my grandmother isn't alive. So am I. She'd be over a hundred now and she wasn't a barrel of fun at sixty. All she ever said to me, when I was five, was I'd pass with a push in a crowd with the light behind me.

Apart from the aforementioned alarums and excursions, I've spent most of the week in the garden, cutting things back. You'd be better occupied, said Josh, cutting Ben back. That boy needs pruning a lot more than apple trees. You know, Mary, I sometimes think second marriages aren't a solution, especially when there are children. Josh and Ben have never been close, but, then, Ben and his real father aren't what you'd call intimate either. Ben said when he went down to Mousehole in the summer he only recognized Tom because who else but his father would be too busy chatting up Britain's only female porter to recognize his son? If that man is my father, said Ben, I think I should be told. I'm such a failure as a woman, Mary, that even biology isn't my destiny.

   Yours, getting me to a nunnery,

   Martha

Martha's mother as instrument of Lenin

Dear Mary

Oh boy, a whole lot of chickens came home to roost here last week. Wait till I tell you, you'll die. First, Daffy Murdoch calls – Daffy Jackson as was. You remember Daffy at school? The one who could hold her breath and make her nostrils click? The one who married the cricketer who must have been kinky about clicking nostrils? We've kept vaguely in touch since her son Godwin – *Godwin* – went to primary school with Ben. Anyhow, Daff says she's got a surprise for me and can she come over for tea? Tea I can't promise, I said, but there's plenty of mashed prunes around here, if you're into scraping them off the ceiling. She wasn't put off. Daffy was always a pushy girl.

So an hour later, there's Daff at the door and just guess who's with her? Old Friz-Chops. Yes, that slice of pressed ham with superfluous hair who sat beside you in the Upper Fourth. And, Mary, Friz-Chops looked *gorgeous*. I mean, as gorgeous as any female can look when she's got a dozen dead seals dripping down her back and a dead lamb perched on her head, which is, I'm sorry to report, pretty gorgeous. Hi hi hi, says Friz-Chops, smiling all over her pearlized lipstick and blowing kisses at me like I'm infectious. Fancy seeing dear Martha Muddle-Brain again! Honestly, isn't it *sad* how some people never grow out of using these infantile labels? Oh, but there was worse to come. Daffy announces that Friz-Chops has just flown over from New York and, Mary, sit down, you're not going to like this, she's just sold her first novel for one million dollars. Bucks, greenbacks, mazumas, lolly.

Now you remember Friz-Chops in English Comp? She couldn't write three words on A Day In The Life Of A Penny without boring us all down the drain. And this PhD in Anaesthetising Plumworth High has written a best-seller? Mary, there is no justice. Oh Martha, she coos, giving phoney little gasps of admiration at the sight of my blitzed kitchen. How cute, how mellow, how laid-back. Look, Friz-Chops, I wanted to say, don't you come in here, oozing your West Coast oil, and think you can get round *me*. Because with *me*, baby, mere money and fame and names in lights cut no ice at all, baby, not even half a cube. I mean, I wouldn't swop a single buck for my wondrous baby and my lovely Jane and my dear-heart Ben.

Just as well I didn't say all that out aloud because it turns out some benighted Wall Street type has hacked his way through the superfluous hair – which is momentarily waxed off – and fathered upon Friz-Chops four little Friz-Chops. Four. Mary, how can people be so irresponsible, in this day and age, as to indulge themselves in four infant carbon copies of Wonderful Them, when half the world is starving? No, it's beyond me, too.

The very cruellest blow of all soon follows. Jane comes in. My heart sinks a bit more because, well, I love Jane but certain women covered in dead animals might be so purblind as to find her a trifle graceless, a mite hoydenish, you know. And what happens? Introduced to Friz-Chops, whom Daffy reveals is known nowadays as Auriol August, Jane goes red all over, says not the Auriol August and asks for her autograph while Friz-Chops simpers. At which, Mary, I wished to be no more. Apparently, Friz-Chops is some sort of feminist heroine to graceless, hoydenish girls like Jane, on account of some non-fiction tract she wrote two years ago about how women put each other down. Have you ever heard of it? The Old School Tithe, I'm told it's called. When Jane's gone, Friz-Chops gushes horribly about what a sweet daughter I've got and aren't they heartening, the young women of today? Heartening? I can feel the first of many angina attacks coming on, if that's what heartening means. OK, Mary, you can get up now and dust yourself off. Isn't it all weird? I mean we were the ones with straight As for Composition at school, you and me. I even got a prize for that essay I wrote which ended 'and the traffic lights turned from red to green and to red again' which was, for a fifteen-year-old, a pretty good way of marking time's passage but where has time's passage actually got me? Josh and a sinkful of dishes is where. I could cry, Mary. I did cry, quite a lot. When Josh came home that night he said Martha, I don't care for that pink eye make-up you're wearing, it doesn't become you. Josh, I said, I don't care for that nose you're wearing. I don't go a bunch on those eyes and that chin and those ears you're wearing, either. Pack 'em in, Josh, or I might just leave for the Big Apple on tonight's Laker standby and sod dinner in the oven.

At the weekend I went to my Women's Centre and, do

Jane meets Auriol August

you know, they are all fans of Auriol August? Auriol? I said. Oh, she's an old mate of mine, we were just like that at school. And she still relies on me for advice and things, does Auriol. She does, Mary. People who've made a lot of money badly need someone like me to keep their feet on the ground. There, said Bess, you see, Martha? You're always saying you're just a housewife but here you are contributing your life experience to someone like Auriol August. Sisterhood is strong, said Bess.

That's so true, Mary. We must stand by each other, who else will? Auriol said, before she left, that any time I wanted to borrow her New York apartment, I'd be welcome. She's obviously trying to say sort of 'thank-you' for, sort of, times gone by, and I appreciate that.

Yours, nostalgically,

Martha

Dear Mary

My back is still aching but wasn't that a great party? About half-way through the day, I felt exactly as if I, personally, had thrown it. Martha, At Home, October 24, Hyde Park or Thereabouts, 11 to 6 pm, CND Banners Will Be Worn. I kept spotting people I hadn't seen for yonks. At Charing Cross, those three lovely Danish women who were at Manchester one year. In Trafalgar Square, Hans-Helmut hanging from a lamppost, that nice German punk I once got stranded with in a train strike. Along Piccadilly, Marie, Lorna's French au pair and then all those women from Birmingham where we stayed on that Women's Conference and guess who, Miss McDonald, our old maths teacher, wheeled down from Edinburgh and still going strong at eighty and the two Liverpudlians who gave us a hitch that time in Brighton and Jenny Cartwright up from Derby and Mrs Next-Door, still laughing herself silly, and Ron from the hairdressers and about thirty people from our street and, oh, about a hundred others. I'm hoarse from catching up with the news, shouting across streets, bellowing over tankards. Marie's had a baby, Kirstie's got married, Manuella from Rome has moved to Paris, Jenny's divorced, it just went on and on.

Going for a sausage roll, I bumped into my own ex-spouse, of all things. Up from Mousehole with a girl called Olly, aged about five and dressed like a Red Indian. I gave her a big hug. Well, she'll need all the hugs she can get, being with Tom. I'm only here for the beer, said Tom, and I believe it. He was more or less legless already and we were only on the Embankment. Look, I said, you come round and see your children before you scuttle back to Cornwall or *else*. I don't know if he got the message – we were parted just then by some street theatre – but, judging by her expression, Olly did. She probably didn't know about her new man's past. I'm the only person Tom is tight-lipped about.

And then, best of all, meeting you! There I was slogging past the Haymarket behind these two huge papier mache figures, Thatcher and Reagan groping each other in the most disgusting way, when out from under them for a breath of fresh air pop you and Mo! We must have held up the hordes for at least six minutes, jumping around. That bloke you were with, the one with the green hair and the gasmask, he was a dish. We met up later, you know. Jammed against the journalists' barricade, under the speakers' platform and from what little he said, ho really fancies you. Then he took his gasmask off and Mary, if you don't fancy him right back, pass him on. What eyes!

He nearly started the only fight of the day though. There were these two journalists in front of us and one said, "Here comes the King," and the other said "You mean, the Prince of Darkness" and we looked up and saw they meant T. Benn. Well, before you could say CND, your bloke was tightening up their ties for nooses. I see why journalists have special barricades – it's to keep them safe from the public.

But it was a downer, coming home. The baby, on my back the whole day without uttering a squeak — obviously he'd only ever needed a quarter of a million other people around to keep him entertained – took one look at home sweet home and began his first bit of serious protest. Josh, who hadn't come on account of he thought Irene might be up in a helicopter and finger him for a fellow-traveller, was sitting there grumbling about how Thatcher was caving in by rescuing the BBC World Service.

What's the point, he complained, financing a lot of frogs, or worse, Englishmen pretending to be Frogs? Joke, he said hastily, seeing my face, but I know enough about that man to know his elaborate jokes merely conceal elaborate truths.

It's like that woman said from the CND platform, Mary. The world is run by old men. Old Reagan, Old Brezhnev and behind them shuffling the papers, Old Josh. Each one sunk in a fantasy of being Gary Cooper in *High Noon* when what they actually are is Count Dracula, back from a good night's necking to keep his cheeks rosy. Josh says I'm paranoic about Cruise etcetera but I say if I'm paranoic, Josh, so is half Europe and how are you going to find a bin big enough to take us all?

Next day, mother phoned and said had I seen all those Communists in London and wasn't it sad. Then an aunt phoned and said had I seen all those Lunatics in London and wasn't it amusing and then Tom appeared, accompanied by Olly. Poor man. I think he's actually afraid of his own children – he looks at them as if they were fireworks gone off at the wrong time. No wonder. Daughter Jane doesn't look

Mrs. Next-Door against the Bomb.

much older than girlfriend Olly, which must be a trifle
unsettling for them all. No good really, using Grecian 2000
and sucking in your beer belly when Jane's around to blow
the gaff.

I wish there was a gardening programme that advised
you about husbands instead of plants. Dear Percy Thrower,
My husbands aren't doing too well. One is curling up at the
edges and losing its leaves and the other has blight. What
should I do? And dear Percy Thrower could tell me to spray
them with derris and all would be well.

Yours, preparing to dig them both over,

Martha

Dear Mary

What is it they say? A son's yours till he marries, but a daughter's a daughter the whole of your life? That makes my future look pretty bleak, I'll tell you, specially as I can't see anyone ever marrying Jane. I mean Jane ever marrying anyone. When I think of all the sleepless nights I've spent soothing her fevered brow, all the days I've slaved over a hot stove cooking her vitamin intake, all the years I've nipped in the bud so she could bloom, sob sob, and here she is turning on me. Holding me up as an object of scorn, looking down at me in my own kitchen, weighing me in the balance and finding me wanting – only Jane could believe *that*, with me going on eleven stone in my stockinged feet. Why do they always say stockinged feet as if women were born with webbed toes, like ducks?

Anyway, Martha, I hear you ask, what could a Saint like you have done to deserve such cruel ingratitude? What I did was buy a copy of *Vogue*. Yes, Mary, *Vogue*. It wasn't easy, either: I stood for ages in front of the rack, perspiring lightly. I read about A.J.P. Taylor's week and how much I'd get for a third-hand Citroen Dyane with body rust and how Saturn was in my Sun sign so I'd better mend my ways and getting goose pimples every time someone came near in case it was Bess or May or some other woman from my Group. In the end I snatched up *Spare Rib*, *Women's Voice*, *New Society*, *New Scientist* and *New Socialist*, stuck *Vogue* well down in the pile, paid and shuffled out with it under plain cover, flat broke. Then, when I'd made it home, I scuttled up to the bathroom, locked myself in and read it. And left it there, forgotten, on account of getting distracted by the ring Ben put around the bath two days ago.

Next thing I know, there's Jane sticking the wretched mag under my nose and saying what's *this*, Martha, in the doomsday voice of someone who's found a cockroach in their soup. Jane, I said, you're old enough now to know the sad truth. Your stepfather is a transvestite with social ambitions. We must be brave and try to help him up the ladder in his Princess of Wales hats.

But she just kept gawping at me, waving the silly mag, so I lost my temper. For heaven's sake I said, or possibly shouted. You caught me bang to rights with the loot. Guv, go easy on me and I'll tell all. No, but *why*, Martha, said Jane. Why schmy I said, or possibly shrieked. Because I'm hooked, that's why. Because I'm a pathetic *Vogue*-ridden wreck of the woman I might have been. You don't know the half of it, Jane. The lost years, trying to kick the habit. The endless weeks at Vogue Anonymous, baring my breast in front of them all, confessing to the Big V. Telling how, at first, I'd only buy one copy now and again, then how I found myself buying more and more, hiding them in my boots, in the cistern, in the freezer, spending the housekeeping, blowing the family allowance. Don't give me Oh Martha, Jane, that's how it was. But I battled. How I battled. I hadn't bought a *Vogue* for a whole year until today, the worst time of the year. Collection Time. Suddenly, the old urge came upon me. I had to know what the hemlines were doing. I *had* to. I staggered down the street to find a pusher, hands trembling, head whirling, and then I blacked out. When I came to, there was a *Vogue* in my handbag. Forgive me, my child, have mercy on your grey-haired mother. With you beside me, I can beat this evil thing. Cut it out, Martha, said Jane.

Good grief, what's so terrible? Have I sold my Sisters down the river for a mess of ready-to-wear? Are women's rights set back a hundred years by my fleeting interest in cinch belts? Will the Sex Discrimination Act fall in tatters because I doled out a quid for the stop-press on cardies. Am I a traitor to feminists everywhere because I want to know what length skirt to buy at Ron's Kooky Klothing, a far yell from Gay Paree.

Thank God for Ben. He came in then in his old black sweater, ancient jeans, and crumbling black boots. Tell you what, I said to him, I'll buy you a whole new outfit, anything you want, name it. Black sweater, jeans, black boots, he said; ta, Mum. Oh, go on, be a devil I said. Have dark grey for a change. You see, Jane? You want a slave to fashion? Meet your brother. Besides, I saw you coming out of Oxfam yesterday, don't think I didn't. We've all got our little habits, my girl, so it ill behoves us to point the finger at others.

Poor old Ben. He and Josh are at loggerheads most of the time these days. Must be something to do with the Primal Hordes – Josh the old stag and Ben getting up his antlers, I don't know. Josh is always nagging him. Don't say no in that negative way, he said to Ben yesterday in one of their set-to's.

How do you say no in a positive way? Or should Ben have said yes in a negative way? Josh obviously feels he's got to give out with the advice all the time too. You know the sort of thing. If you had more cold showers, Ben, your teeth wouldn't ache. If you stood up straight and put your shoulders back, we wouldn't have to leave the Common Market. If you ran round the block every morning, Sadat would be alive today. Helpful stuff like that.

Josh came in just now and said what's for dinner, Martha? Fried cholesterol, I said.

Yours, spoiling for a mixed grill,

Martha

Dear Mary

You didn't mention my Vogue true confessions in your reply – does that mean you found them too abhorrent to dwell on or has the Post Office had another of its hiccups? Perhaps you've been side-tracked by true love at last? That bloke I got crushed up against the CND platform with, is he – you know – your bloke? From what I gather, you seem to talk about nothing, together, but NATO Contingency Plans and the ethos of Flexible Response but what your friends want to know is, have you gone Critical yet? And, if so, do you have Manouvreable Re-entry Vehicles (MARV) or are you still using Terrain Comparison (TERCOM)? Only asking.

We had our own limited strategic flare-up last night, it being Guy Fawkes. Ben conned me out of a small fortune for fireworks and we went over to Lorna's so he and Lorna's son Zep could let them off in Lorna's back garden. Our garden was out due to Josh going through his papers again and accusing Ben of wishing to ignite a deeply important Fiscal Green Paper with an indoor sparkler. Lorna and I spent most of the time yelling through the windows at the boys – they kept bending over their Catherine Wheels in a horribly dangerous way. I ended up with a sore throat, shouting Ben, if you go blind, don't think you're coming in here again (what did I plan, to keep him stumbling about in the garden all his life?) while Lorna shrieked incessantly watch out, you idiots, or it'll be White Stick time for you.

The fireworks were lovely, though. I said to Lorna that if I were rich, I'd have them going all the time, like medieval torches in my public rooms. Lorna said she thought it'd really suit me if my hair caught fire. That sulphurous flare does a lot for your skin, she said.

Sometimes I think that woman lacks all human emotion. After the fireworks, she and I were sampling her drinks cupboard – full of holiday leftovers like Basque liqueur and Occitane aperitifs and sticky Greek ouzo – when she tells me her mother is dying and would I go and see her? Lorna, I said, one thing a friend can't do for a friend is visit a friend's dying

mother. Dying mothers don't want to see perfect strangers, they want to see daughters. Mine doesn't, said Lorna. She's always said she doesn't want me at her deathbed because I'm the sort of person who would try to steal the limelight from anyone, even on their deathbeds.

Apparently, Lorna's mother was once a vaudeville artiste called Queenie King and led Lorna a difficult childhood. She gave a party, once, backstage, when Lorna was a baby, covered her all over with the guests' fur coats and forgot about her for the rest of the evening. Lorna was dug out at 3 am suffering from oxygen deprivation, which may account for her lack of a fully developed emotional life to this day. When Queenie first started on the downward spiral, Lorna would phone me and say could I give Zep his supper because her mum had take up her natural position again – flat on her back on the floor, surrounded by broken bottles. Lorna's spent the past three years committing her, and doctors have spent the past three years uncommitting her, because of the Cuts. That woman goes in and out of bins like plastic liners.

Have just heard the news about Princess Di's baby. Lorna says poor ducky, she'll have to have a Caesarean on account of the ears, which is typical of her unfeeling approach to the rich tapestry of human life. I think it's nice news. Heaven knows, I'll never have a grandchild, due to Jane refusing to be in the same room with any man apart from Rover, who refuses to be in the same room with Jane, and Ben being in love with carburettors and women too old to reproduce, like Wendy. I do envy pregnant women – it's the only time in your life you can do absolutely nothing and know you're doing something.

My heart sank yesterday. Delia Smith's put her Christmas Pudding recipe in the paper again, which means only six weeks' dithering time to the dreaded 25th again. Mother has already rung, like Christmas bells, to ask what my plans are, which is her way of saying she'll be catching the 4.45 pm on December 24 and will we please meet her at Victoria.

Martha

Dear Mary

I'm sitting here at the kitchen table, dead tired, in my dressing-gown, yawning my head off, all ready for beddy-byes and it's just gone 9 am. Ben's departed for school leaving note saying It Was Not Me Took the Creem Off of the Milk and Jane's departed for college leaving empty tins of oxtail soup behind her. Can oxtail soup be called a proper breakfast? What *is* an ox? Surely they don't grow in England? The poor creatures are probably shipped from India or somewhere, tails and all, in ghastly freighters, mooing. Or whatever oxes do. The baby is down on the floor with the cat eating Whiskas – he's particularly partial to the Lamb's Heart flavour – and Josh banged the door quite loudly as he went off to the office, saying all he ever wanted for breakfast was one bowl of Sultana Bran and why was there never any or was that too much to ask of a liberated wife?

Reading about the Russian submarine in Swedish waters had set his adrenalin seething. You see, Martha? He said. There's your peace-loving Soviets for you, floating missile bases skulking about under other people's seas, so much for your woolly CNDers. I must say I do *wish* the Russians would listen to my advice. The fact that they don't is I must admit, one of their least attractive features.

The news in general this week has packed some of the bags under my eyes. First, after that doctor gets cleared of murdering the baby, we're confronted with two hundred articles about how we're now only one step away from the gas chambers and me hardly able to cope with my perfectly healthy, presumably normal infant. Like that awful old prune Mugg who, I bet, has never so much as stuffed a teaspoonful of groats in a child's mouth, going on about legislation opening doors through which we'll soon be pushing those without whom we might appear to be better off. Such as that awful old prune Mugg, I say, and wish I hadn't.

Why is it that people who are against everything you believe in always make you react in exactly the way they're arguing? Why do I always want to kill everyone who wants to kill everyone? Then there's all that about spies, how they've given immunity to this spy and that spy so's they can track down some other spy. Perhaps these confessions will eventually lead to the uncovering of one really Enormous Spy, a sort of vast multi-national Spy's Spy, the Hundredth Man, entirely covered with micro-dots and poison-tipped umbrellas and so camp he can hardly walk.

And then there's the business about loyalty in the Labour Party. Funny, that. Josh is always on about loyalty, too. The thing is, people who want your loyalty inevitably mean 'in spite of' what you really believe. So being loyal always means going against your conscience or concealing your deepest beliefs or whatever. Otherwise, they wouldn't have to ask. Josh says I should be more loyal whenever I ask what he really *does* in the Department – ie shut up, do what you're told, them that ask no questions get told no lies. At his last office party, he put his arm round my shoulder said this is my loyal little wife, Martha, and I had an instant attack of the Anthony Blunts.

By the way, Josh has announced that we have to give a party before Christmas, we owe so many people. He may, I don't – I only know two people. I can't hardly recall the last real party I went to, while Josh is always having drinkies after work with his mates. I suggested we hire a hall or a pub or something but Josh said never, people expect to come to your house for hospitality. There's nothing hospitable about our house, I said, unless you think peeling wallpaper and sofas covered in cat's hair hospitable but he was adamant. So I'm going to throw a Come As You Aren't party. I shall appear as a female executive in T bar shoes and I'll dress Jane up as Miss World and Irene will arrive in curlers and a pinny and you can take everything off and come as a sex symbol and Mother can be a doormat.

Mind you, it might bring on Josh's incipient identity crisis. He's obviously none too sure who he is, always leafing through his Diner's Club catalogues, yearning for cuff-links and shirts and bathrobes with his initals on. Do you anticipate becoming an amnesiac shortly? I said to him. Losing your memory and waving initialled hankies at concerned coppers? He wasn't amused but, then, he rarely is, these days, poor man. Sometimes I feel so sorry for him. He wanted a wife and a baby and he even quite fancied the idea of ready-made kiddies like Jane and Ben but none of us, I'm afraid, have come up to expectation, especially not when compared to Diner's Club families. If he'd ordered us on spec, we'd all have been returned by now, without obligation.

I know he envisaged me in a hostess gown, waiting for him at the door with a mixed Martini and the baby, flushed and rosy and quiet in Nanny's arms and Jane, pretty as a picture in broderie anglaise, hanging on his every word, and Ben frightfully intelligent in pebble glasses, asking for advice, and our only real problem the shortage of schools for extremely gifted children. Instead of which . . well, I won't go into that, it's too depressing. I had a different picture of him, too, but I mind much more that we disappoint him than that he disappoints us, I don't know why. I do try, now and again. I painted my nails on Monday but by Tuesday the bits were flaking into the fishcakes and Josh said it was unhygienic.

Yours, face down in the Kelloggs,

Martha

Josh's
vision.

Dear Mary

Here is a wee snatch of seasonal verse for you:

Ortum leaves are tumbling down
To fertalize the sogy groun

I found it in Ben's pocket. With any luck, it isn't his. I can't tell his handwriting because it drifts in a different direction every day. Like ortum leaves. And Jane's been nagging me about Rover. He's got nowhere to spend Christmas, she says, so what am I going to do about it? I say that Christmas is a time for taking in frail old ladies, not huge Mr Universes who will eat the whole turkey and all the mince pies while trying to catch glimpses of their beautiful selves in the Christmas tree baubles. Besides, Rover's living with his auntie down the road, so what about her? She's Jewish, says Jane. In that case, I point out patiently, Rover's Jewish and won't want anything to do with Christmas, anyway. Rover, says Jane, is not Jewish because he. Then she goes very red. Because he *what*? I say, steely-voiced. Because he, she repeats and suddenly discovers she is extremely late for an extremely pressing appointment and shoots off. Leaving me with nothing but suspicions darkening my door.

Only a month ago I was forced to have a talk with Ben, after he and his geriatric girl-friend Wendy had spent about 15 hours sealed in his bedroom with a padlock on the door and a notice saying Keap Out This Meens You. Josh wouldn't have a talk with him. Josh said let Tom have a talk with him and I said what? The facts of life through a megaphone from Mousehole? Anyway, I've got Jane and Ben to prove that what their father knows about you-know-what could be put on the end of a you-know-what. So I said to Ben, if you're you-know-whating with Wendy I only hope you're you-know-what. What? said Ben. Well, I said, is Wendy on the thingummy, that's what. Yes, said Ben. Are you sure? I said. Sure, he said. I see her take it just before.

And now I've got Jane to worry about. She knows all about you-know-what and thingummies, of course, but what's she doing about it? I suppose I'll have to have a talk with her now, too. One thing about me, though, Mary. I'm absolutely out front with the kids about you-know-what and thingummies and so on. As a parent, I consider that essential, nowadays.

Because of this awful Christmas party Josh says I've got to give, I went out and bought myself an address book and all that's done is reveal on a hundred empty pages what I already knew. I don't know anybody. I've got you and Mo and Mother down and my American friend and Auriol August the Famous Feminist Author, to add tone, and that's it. I don't know the addresses of people I actually see, like Bess and May and Lorna and, anyway, that's only eight out of the population of the world, which is probably too minute a percentage for a computer to calculate. To compensate, I started to cut things out of the papers and magazines. In the end, I said to Josh, look, I've got a really efficient address book together now. If you ever need to know, there's everyone here from the Art Work Director of Gay Collective Digest to the Deputy Under Secretary at the UK Embassy in Qatar. Same man, I shouldn't wonder, said Josh.

By the way, why are you and Mo going on that March for Jobs? I mean, someone might give you one and then what would you do? I know it's the principle that matters and everything and I don't want to be rude but Mo with her purple hair doesn't come across as the world's most instantly employable person and the last time I saw her on a demo she was holding a banner saying I Won't Be A Wage Slave. I will. Or, at least, I'd rather be a Wage Slave than a No-Wage Slave, which is what I am now.

I know you keep saying I'm earning the money Josh gives me (I mean pays me) and I know I am, too, but does he? I wish the Department would send the housekeeping in a nice computer-printed brown envelope, so I wouldn't have to thank Josh. At the moment, I just sort of snatch the notes awkwardly but the words 'thank you' will keep leaking through my teeth. It isn't that I mind thanking him that much, only it gives Josh the wrong impression. Lorna goes to extremes. She gets her old man to push the money through the letterbox and she picks it up from the mat. That's silly, Lorna, I said when she told me. Silly heck she said. The Medium, Martha, is the Message. Perhaps she's right. The only wages I get for myself these days is when I post off the coupons that come in my ciggies. I get ever so excited when the money comes back but there must be easier ways of earning a living than tarring up your lungs smoking 200 fags for a pound.

Lastly but not leastly, yes, of course I'll be there as your character witness when you come up for pillaging that porn shop but for goodness sake, watch yourself. It'll be no good at all me going on about how your father was this deeply wonderful General who killed half a hundredweight of people in wars and other background info judges like to hear if you're effing away in the dock. And do remember, judges dress funny so you must, too. Borrow a modest black number from someone, put some Cherry Blossom pearlized lipstick on, and don't say Old Bill or anything *at all* about women's lib. Just come on like you're a respectable virgin lady who had a sudden turn as she passed the dreaded Spot because it sullied all you hold dear, including the sacred memory of your mother who died on active service with Mothers For The Bomb. One thing more, *don't* plead PMT or they'll prove you're on the Pill and haven't had a PM to be T about since two days cum Tuesday last Michaelmas.

Yours, packing twin-set and pearls,

Martha

GIVE

Lorna's system.

Dear Mary

The morning after I got back from you, I came down stairs, put All-Bran in my tea-cup, poured boiling water on it and nearly choked to death. Then I went upstairs and came down again, to have another go at starting the day. All your fault. Mercy may descend on young and single women as the gentle rain but on me, a middle-aged wife and mother, it falleth as a concrete brick from heaven. The magistrate lets you and Mo off with nothing but a warning, thanks to me perjuring myself silly in the witness box, but who's around to speak up for me when I get home and find Josh pronouncing the death sentence, suspended only so long as I do not stir from the broom cupboard for the rest of my wedded life?

Naturally, I hadn't told him of my starring role at Sebastopol Magistrates' Court. Apart from anything else, I'd reckoned on being home and dry before he'd got himself and his papers shovelled out the office door. As it was, I made it on the stroke of midnight, swaying very slightly from the effects of our celebratory substances, and oh wow, did this Cindrella hit rag-time. If there's one thing Josh cannot abide, it's me being out of the house when he comes home and, in case you think that's touching, the other thing he cannot abide is me being in the house when he comes home. He's always said Away-Day tickets proved British Rail is run by Reds to lure wives from their marital duties. Now, he knows.

Your Mother phoned while you were gone, he said, among other things. She was very worried. She said she had never permitted herself to leave you when you were young but that was, of course, before Women's Lib. I had to lie to her, Martha, for your sake. I had to say you'd gone to nurse a sick friend. I didn't leave my young, I said. Who d'you think this is? And I stuck the baby in his arms, to keep them still. Shove Mother anyway, I said. That woman got Power of Attorney from God to make her family as miserable as possible in His Name. My poor old Dad couldn't smoke or drink because Mother's friend God was a non-smoking teetotaller, not to mention a non-you-know-whatter, and what was good enough for Him was good enough for my Dad. How I got born at all is a secret to this day between Him and her. At any rate, Dad was never consulted.

But defending yourself only gives you a headache and you don't get legal aid. Next day, the polyunsaturated fat really hit the fire. Irene, she of the nuclear hairstyle, charges into Josh's office waving a copy of your local rag, the *Sebastopol Clarion*. Heaven knows how it got into her clammy hands; smuggled down a thin blue line from a Moral Majority cell at the bottom of your road, I suppose. And there, on the front page, was a blotchy likeness of you and me outside the Court, headlined 'Bra-Burners Warned in Porn Shop Plunder'.

This, of course, confirmed Irene in her worst fears of me. Now she thinks I'm the Mrs Big in some sleazy Copenhagen Connection, aided and abetted by a delinquent baby. Josh did me no good at all by saying oh god, this time Martha's gone too far. A most unsavoury business, Josh, said Irene. Not *at all* the sort of thing the Department expects of Department Wives. And she swept out, squashing underfoot, on her way, most of Josh's promotion prospects.

I did try to make Josh understand. Look, I said, when that old school friend of yours, Woolly Something, came up on a charge of doing beastly things in bushes, you did your bit for him in Court. That, said Josh, was entirely different and, besides, it was a ridiculous charge and, besides, the magistrate was old Bendy Baxter who knew as well as I did that old Woolly had *always* done beastly things in bushes, so what was the good of sending him to prison and setting a bad example to the criminal classes? Talk about male bonding.

Well, what can I do to make it better? I said. If I ring Irene to explain, I'll only get her under-secretary and have to leave a message so garbled she'll think she's had an obscene phone call and get above herself. Anyway, Josh, Mary and Mo weren't doing anything beastly like Woolly. They were trying to stop pornographers degrading women. And you know what my husband said? He said wake up, Martha, be realistic. Who do you *expect* pornographers to degrade? Budgies? Wake up? I haven't closed an eyelid since. Why is it that whenever the Women's Movement strikes, it's my foundations that wobble, not yours? Is that fair, Mary? Where's the Retirement Home for Distressed Ungentlewomen, not to mention their sex-war-shocked Issue?

Still, what can I do but soldier on and pretend I can't see the cracks? Our party, in case your recent legal triumph has wiped it from your mind, is next Thursday. On second thoughts, stay with the wiped mind. The thing's going to be a disaster, anyway. Ben did the invitations for me and wrote 'Drinks at Moon' on them all so the guests'll turn up at 12 midnight instead, or the barmy ones will. I'm too depressed to care.

Kev came in an hour ago with the bloke he'd said he'd find to repair the fridge. This is Merv, Marf, said Kev. Merv'll see you right. Merv didn't. Merv's just gone, leaving the fridge and me broken down. Remember old Paddy, Marf? says Merv. Sad about old Paddy. Took a clot on the brain, down the Star and Garter, not been the same since. Know young Joe, Marf? Bad about Joe. Come down with his lungs something rotten, wouldn't recognize him. Seen old Mrs Collop, Marf? No, you wouldn't. Took to her bed with the kidneys, August, she won't be up again. Remember Irish Ted, Marf . . .?

Yours, gone down with the mouth,

Marf

Irene points out item of interest to old and broken man.

Dear Mary

Not a squeak out of you since you stumbled into the night with Rover ranged round your shoulders like a giant stole. Range Rover. Did you get caught in his medallions and have to check into casualty to have him surgically removed? He wasn't supposed to *be* at the party – Jane smuggled him in. Now she's locked in her bedroom shouting 'just resting' to all inquiries, like an out-of-work actress.

Mary, you did *understand* about Rover? He has to be gay, and choosey with it, mostly choosing himself. Jane's still young enough to think she could be the light on his road to Damascus but you and I know different, don't we? Yet why no word? If Rover were a *normal* man, I'd have called in the police by now to drag the canal for your body.

It took me three days' work to prepare for that party. Just moving the sofas back revealed enough cats' hairs to knit another cat. The one I've got moped about for a while in the melee and then fainted. She always faints when she feels she's being ignored. I dropped her on Josh's lap (laps being things people have who aren't pulling their weight) and she spent the next hour licking his hair, under the impression that she'd found her long lost kitten. I wouldn't lick Josh's hair, and I'm married to him.

Bess popped in to give me a hand, along with some child she was minding. He's a bit *disturbed*, she whispered. I can tell that, I whispered back, he's done exactly what he's told since he came in. Unlike Ben, who is, of course, perfectly undisturbed. To prove it, he ate every second canape we made, walked round and round and *round* the kitchen table as if he thought, keep this up long enough and that table will play a tune and, later on, had to be put to bed by Studs after swigging the wine he was supposed to be passing around. Studs said Ben's last words, before flaking out, were 'when do we get to Calais?'

Mother came in to help, too. Mother's help consisted of standing at my elbow saying I wouldn't do *that*, dear, if I were you but, then, when did you ever listen to your Mother?

Also getting cups of tea for Josh, clucking. Which, interpreted, means how much better off you'd be, poor boy, if I were your wife instead of *her*. Well, there's only eight years and Mother's hats between them, so I wish them all the luck in the world.

Then Merv and Kev turned up, delivering our crates of wine which they kindly proceeded to unpack, mostly down their gullets. Cheers Marf, they'd say, each time I looked their way. Cheers Merv, I'd say. Cheers Kev. With hindsight, those cheers were my undoing. Josh kept shooting sidelong glances at me, the kind Chinese waiters give when you're eating late, like they could just restrain themselves by some Oriental isometrics from plunging a dagger in your heart. Keep stroking the cat, Josh, I said. Cheers.

At some point the door bell rang and the party was off. On. In bounced the Tinkerton-Smiths, fuelled by marital discord, their specs alight with mutual hatred. In leaned Nigel and Caroline, him backwards, her forwards. In swayed Irene carefully balancing her hair on her head like a seal with a ball. A Departmental Venus surrounded by waves of pinstripes all saying wonderful and very true and *there* you are, Josh, *jolly* good. In came Lorna with her mother Queenie, risen from her sickbed for the occasion. Queenie had to be unhooked from one of the pinstripes later – it's not that I think women are too old for sex at 75, but shouldn't they wait to be asked? Or is Queenie the earliest known specimen of Femina Liberata?

And there were you and Mo, along with those five unisex persons covered in badges saying 'I love Wimmin'. So do we, har har, chorused the pinstripes, and got sardines stuffed in their buttonholes for their pains. Mother said to me, Martha, Mo is *charming*. She may look a little eccentric but she's got her priorities right, not like *some* I could mention. So I asked Mo what she'd been on about to Mother. Just told your old lady how me and Mare gave that shop a good dusting over, said Mo. Halfway through, Auriol August mainfested herself, entirely covered with furry mammals, and Josh disappeared with her for some time, to show her his etchings. Being Josh, he actually has some. And I consoled myself with a dear little man called Carruthers. Well, he must have another name but I prefer Carruthers. Down, Carruthers, I said at one point. I *am* down, he said. So sweet. I think he's taken quite a shine to me or, at least, to the parts of me he's met.

About midnight, Irene came at me through the smokey

haze with her tongue out. This is it, I thought. Confrontation time. Then I saw the tongue was bleeding and, in a flash, remembered that jar of olives Jane had broken on the way home. I did think we'd got all the glass out with rinsing. What'll I do, I asked myself, if she falls down dead from powdered glass? Will I be arrested for murder, like a Victorian jealous wife? I covered up well, though, you would have been proud of me. Looks like scurvy to me, Irene, I said, are you getting enough vitamin C? Have an orange, do. Have two. But I needed a good few stiff ones after that, I can tell you. I don't recall much more of the party. Josh says I sang three verses of Knocked 'em in the Old Kent Road and collapsed, to the giggles of Mrs Next-Door which, added to her usual menopausal giggles, rendered her more or less uncontrollable.

The morning after, Josh announced that he'd come to the end of his tether. Tether? I said. What's a tether when it's at home? Put your tether in triplicate, Josh, and get Irene to sign it and I'll give it due consideration.

Yours, at the end of something or other,

Martha